DOUGLAS - LAXEY - RAMSEY

Tom Heavyside

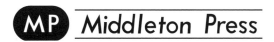

MP Middleton Press

Front cover: Manx Electric Railway 'Tunnel Car' no.7, built 1894, is at Laxey on 8th May 1997. The Snaefell Mountain Railway tracks are on the left. (T.Heavyside)

Back cover upper: Snaefell Mountain Railway no.1, built 1895, begins the descent of the Laxey Valley from the Bungalow on 11th May 2000. The lever in the foreground switches the crossover points. This is normally only used during the TT races when cars terminate here. (T.Heavyside)

Back cover lower: This is a nocturnal scene at Lhen Coan, Groudle Glen Railway, on 19th August 1998. Today the veteran 2-4-0T Sea Lion *(left), which first worked here back in 1896, is ably assisted by 0-4-2T* Annie *built in 1997. (T.Heavyside)*

ACKNOWLEDGEMENTS

In addition to those mentioned in the photographic credits much valued assistance has been received from P.Abell, M.Bairstow, P.Barber, Rev P.Brew, P.Cannel, R.Carpenter, R.M.Casserley, B.Darvill, R.Dodge, E.Gray, E.Johnson, T.Nall, D.J.Porter, A.Scarffe, K.Smith, H.Stevenson, G.Taylor and T.Wilson. I am also indebted to A.Frankland and the staff at the Manx Museum Library in Douglas and to R.K.Hateley for drawing the map of the island, the gradient profiles and the track plans. Again, my sincere thanks to everyone.

Published July 2010

ISBN 978 1 906008 75 8

© Middleton Press, 2010

Design Deborah Esher

Published by
        Middleton Press
        Easebourne Lane
        Midhurst
        West Sussex
        GU29 9AZ
Tel: 01730 813169
Fax: 01730 812601
Email: info@middletonpress.co.uk
www.middletonpress.co.uk

Printed in the United Kingdom by Henry Ling Limited, at the Dorset Press, Dorchester, DT1 1HD

CONTENTS

I.   Map of the Isle of Man showing the railway network at its zenith. For clarity only the main stopping places on the Manx Electric Railway are marked.

INDEX

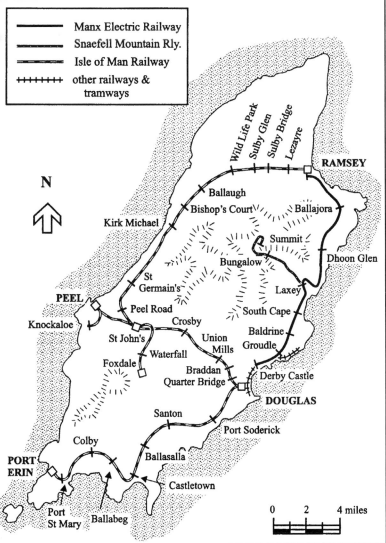

GEOGRAPHICAL SETTING

The Isle of Man is surrounded by the Irish Sea. As the crow flies, from its most northerly point to the southern tip is a distance of 30 miles, while its eastern and western coasts are never more than 10 miles apart.

The principal port and capital of the island, Douglas, is situated where the waters of the rivers Dhoo and Glass combine before flowing into the sea, at the edge of the Eastern Coastal Plateau. Ramsey, the second largest town located some 15 miles to the north, lies by the mouth of the River Sulby at the south-east corner of the Northern Plain. The high mountainous area of the Northern Upland Massif separates the two towns and, north of Laxey, extends up to the eastern seaboard. The coastline is punctuated by a number of deep glens running inland.

Derby Castle, where the main part of our journey commences, is situated at the north end of Douglas Promenade. From here the Manx Electric Railway negotiates a meandering, switchback, 17¾-mile route through some very difficult terrain by way of Groudle, Laxey, Dhoon and Ballajora before finally reaching the town centre of Ramsey. There are a number of long, steep inclines, the 2¾-mile length starting just outside Laxey up to the summit of the line at 588ft above sea level, between Bulgham Bay and Dhoon Glen, being particularly taxing, with successive sections graded at 1 in 38/27/28 and 24. In parts the line passes through some pleasant rolling countryside, while in other areas it overlooks various glens or runs close to the coastline. When conditions are favourable, from numerous locations, parts of Cumbria and south-west Scotland are clearly visible across the open sea, while on the landward side the high rising ground to the west is never very far away.

A bed of Manx slate lies beneath the entire route with some granite deposits in the Dhoon area, while lead and zinc ore was once mined at Laxey.

III. Gradient profile Derby Castle to Ramsey.

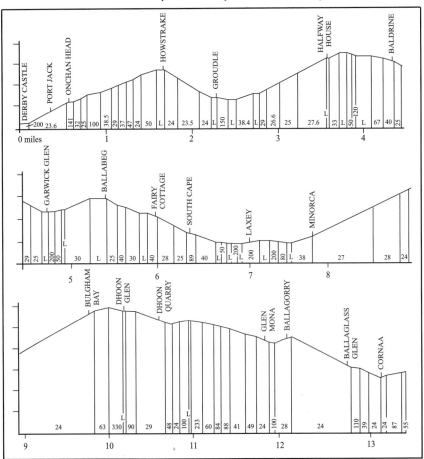

HISTORICAL BACKGROUND

Between August 1876 and July 1890, a 1½-mile 3ft 0in gauge horse tramway, originally promoted by 'comeover' Thomas Lightfoot, was opened in stages along Douglas Promenade, between the ferry terminal and Derby Castle. Hardly had this been completed when, with the island growing in popularity as a tourist destination, under the Howstrake Estate Act of 1892 the Douglas & Laxey Coast Electric Tramway Company was incorporated to promote a 3ft 0in gauge tramway north along the east coast. A single line section from Derby Castle to Groudle was officially opened on 7th September 1893, before closing at the end of the month for the winter.

The next year, on 1st May 1894, the D&LCETCo purchased the Douglas Horse Tramway (the latter having been owned by Isle of Man Tramways Ltd since 1882) whereupon it changed its name to the Isle of Man Tramways & Electric Power Co Ltd. The line as far as Groudle reopened on 12th May 1894, the track in the interim having been doubled, cars continuing onwards to the first Laxey station, near the site of the present car shed, from 28th July of the same year. Two years later a new terminus at Laxey was opened on the south side of Glen Roy. Meanwhile, at the end of 1895, the company had acquired the electrified Snaefell Mountain Railway, the history of the two lines being closely allied thereafter.

A further Act of Tynwald (the Manx Government), passed on 13th May 1897, authorised the construction of a line north from Laxey to Ramsey, services commencing to Ballure, on the southern outskirts of the town, on 2nd August 1898. The extension was closed for the winter on 24th October and reopened the following 17th June, cars being able to carry passengers into the town centre of Ramsey from 24th July 1899, although mail had been collected from the new terminus for a couple of weeks beforehand.

Not long after this, in February 1900, due to a large debt that it could not repay, the IoMT&EPCo became heavily embroiled in the infamous collapse of Dumbell's Bank, a closure that caused financial havoc throughout the island. Eventually, in September 1901, the liquidator sold the Douglas Horse Tramway to Douglas Corporation, with a new company, the Manx Electric Railway, securing both the coastal and Snaefell lines in November 1902. Over the ensuing years the fortunes of these concerns has ebbed and flowed, generally in line with those of the tourist industry.

Following a particularly difficult period for the railways during the early to mid-1950s, principally due to the falling numbers of visitors attracted to the island, control of the MER, including the Snaefell Mountain Railway, was transferred to the Government on 1st June 1957. However, under nationalisation the problems continued unabated, and in March 1975 Tynwald took the contentious decision to close the MER north of Laxey from 1st October on a permanent basis, with the southern section being retained for use during the summer months only.

Subsequent to a change of Government at the November 1976 elections, it was decided to reinstate the service through to Ramsey, this officially reopening on 25th June 1977. The following year the Manx Electric Railway Board also became responsible for the Isle of Man Steam Railway, after this too had been nationalised (see *Douglas to Port Erin*). For three years from 1983, the railways, along with the buses, were administered by the Isle of Man Passenger Transport Board. Since 1986 the Government-owned transport undertakings have been an integral part of the Department of Tourism & Transport, and as well as providing a service for residents, the various railways are acknowledged as important tourist attractions.

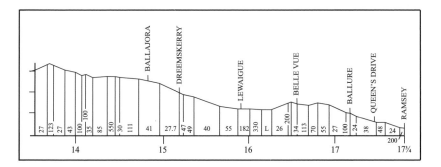

PASSENGER SERVICES

When services were inaugurated through to the centre of Ramsey in the summer of 1899, cars left Douglas Derby Castle at half-hourly intervals from 7am to 9pm on weekdays and from 9.30am to 8pm on Sundays.

Listed below are the total number of departures scheduled to leave Derby Castle for Ramsey during the peak summer months for a few selected years.

Year	Weekdays	Sundays
1906	24	17
1934	19	12
1943	11	4
1966	17	12
1983	17	10
1995	13	10

On Saturdays there was usually an additional late evening service.

Often, in the past, a footnote to the published timetables stated 'extra cars will also run between the advertised times as required by traffic'. In practice, on high days, to cope with demand a much more frequent service operated between Derby Castle and Laxey, while other cars turned back at Onchan, Groudle, or Garwick. On occasions cars have been known to leave Derby Castle at 5min intervals.

Due to the seasonal nature of the tourist trade, a reduced service has usually operated at the shoulders of the main season with a basic hourly pattern in winter. In days gone by, throughout the year some journeys were timed to connect with the steamers departing or arriving at Douglas Harbour, these being denoted as 'Boat Cars' in the timetable. Other services carried mail.

In recent times the service has been sparser than in days of yore, with normally no early morning or evening journeys possible except for a limited Derby Castle to Groudle shuttle on days when the Groudle Glen Railway has been open of an evening. In 2010 services were scheduled from mid-March until the beginning of November, and depending on seasonal demands, the number from Derby Castle through to Ramsey varied between four and thirteen, augmented at times by some to Laxey only. A new feature was an evening service to Laxey on certain Wednesday evenings to connect with cars on the Snaefell Mountain Railway. The 24 hour clock was adopted in 2000.

Currently there are no less than 69 designated stopping places, although most are 'request stops', many of which are little used. Those illustrated are marked on the gradient profile. Journey time between Douglas and Ramsey is 1 hour 15 minutes.

POWER CARS

In total 32 power cars were imported from England between 1893 and 1906. The first three, open-ended nos 1 to 3, were shipped across the Irish Sea from G.F.Milnes & Co Ltd of Birkenhead (the company having previously supplied cars to the horse tramway) in time for the opening of the line from Derby Castle to Groudle in September 1893. As built they were powered by two Mather & Platt Ltd of Manchester 25hp motors, current from the overhead wire, energised at 500 volts dc, being collected by means of two rigid John Hopkinson patent bow collectors. They could carry up to 38 passengers (later officially reduced to 36) on longitudinal seats.

Nos 4 to 9 with vestibules at each end and seats for 34 people (no.5 later reconfigured for 32) arrived from Milnes the following year. The current was received by means of new improved spring bows patented by Edward Hopkinson, brother of John. Also they were slightly narrower than nos 1 to 3 and on account of this are usually referred to as 'Tunnel Cars'.

Four more vestibuled cars, nos 10 to 13, with slightly different dimensions to their predecessors, were purchased from Milnes in 1895, this time kitted out for 46 passengers, 40 on transverse reversible seats plus another three fixed in each bulkhead. As passenger carriers they had a very short existence, all being withdrawn by 1903, before they were converted for the carriage of freight or cattle.

With the opening of the extension from Laxey to Ramsey in 1898 extra cars were needed and that year a further nine bodies were supplied by Milnes. These had glazed bulkheads and a clerestory roof but open sides with cross bench seating for 56 passengers. Five, nos 14 to 18, were fitted with four 20hp motors supplied by Electric Construction Company of Wolverhampton together with more conventional trolley poles, the Hopkinson bows on the earlier cars also being replaced by poles about this time. The other four bodies initially entered service as trailers. Side roller shutters were installed a few years later for the protection of passengers during inclement weather.

The next year, 1899, the four 'Winter Saloons' emerged from Milnes factory, powered at first by Electric Construction motors. Numbered 19 to 22, these 37ft 6in long, 7ft 4in wide cars were the largest built for the railway. Fully glazed with transverse double seats for 40 plus a triple and single seat in each bulkhead, they have proved highly suitable for use throughout the year.

No.23 was a centre-cab locomotive built by the Isle of Man Tramways & Electric Power Company themselves at Derby Castle in 1900 for freight haulage. When required it ran on borrowed bogies, usually from no.17, and thus at peak periods had perforce to stand idle. It was withdrawn in January 1914 following an accident, but was rebuilt in 1925 on a new underframe with two wagon bodies mounted either side of the cab. As before, when needed, bogies off other cars were used, often from no.33.

In 1903, as part of a major re-equipment programme, the other four bodies received from Milnes in 1898, then running as nos 40 to 43, were converted to power cars, this time using Brush bogies and four 25hp motors by Belgium manufacturer Société l'Electricité et l'Hydraulique. In order to accommodate the wider Brush bogies it was necessary to raise the footboards at each end. On completion they were renumbered 24 to 27. The same year, no.16 similarly received Brush bogies and Belgium motors together with modified footboards, the quintet quickly being nicknamed 'Paddleboxes'.

With more cars still needed the company then turned to the Electric Railway & Tramway Carriage Works Ltd of Preston who supplied cars nos 28 to 31 in 1904. These 56-seat cross bench opens were very similar to those received from Milnes in 1898, but with J.G.Brill of Philadelphia bogies and four outside-hung 25hp motors by Société l'Electricité et l'Hydraulique. By the end of the year the improved running gear on these four cars had been exchanged with that fitted to the 'Winter Saloons'. The air braking system was also removed from nos 28 to 31, the quartet subsequently having to rely solely on the hand brake mechanism. Because of this they were quickly dubbed 'Ratchet Cars'.

The last of the cars ordered by the Manx Electric Railway, nos 32 and 33, were despatched to the island from Preston in 1906, having been put together by the United Electric Car Co Ltd, who by then had taken over ER&TCW. The main difference to those supplied in 1904 was the use of four 27½hp motors by General Electric. With a total of 110hp available they were thus the most powerful cars in the fleet.

In addition, during the years to 1906, various cheques were handed over to the makers of the power cars for 29 trailers. Always numbered in sequence after the power cars, so as to avoid clashes as the latter increased it became necessary to renumber the trailers, some having four different identities during their early years. They were finally allocated nos 34 to 62.

Over the years many modifications and improvements have been made to the stock, far too many to detail here. Quite remarkably, even though some have not turned a wheel for many years, apart from nos 10 to 13 and five due to fire, none of the others have ever officially been condemned. Nos 3, 4, 8 and 24 were lost, along with seven trailers, in the inferno that engulfed Laxey car shed on the evening of Saturday 5th April 1930, and similarly the body of no.22 was destroyed in a fire at Derby Castle in September 1990. The latter returned to service two years later with a new body.

The only additions to stock since 1906 have been three trailers by English Electric of Preston in 1930 as replacements for some of those written-off at Laxey earlier that year and the replica 3ft 6in gauge Snaefell Mountain Railway freight car no.7 'Maria' in 2003. The latter has since been regauged to 3ft 0in and fitted with a diesel engine, emerging from Derby Castle as no.34 in 2008. The former no.34 was one of the trailers destroyed in the Laxey fire in 1930.

As regards liveries, it is understood initially Prussian blue figured prominently, but combinations of red, brown and cream soon became the standard. Thereafter the only main variation came about following the takeover by the Government in 1957 when a start was made on repainting the cars green and white. This proved very unpopular with the traditional colours being restored by 1963. In more recent years a few of the cars have sported historic identities, while for a short time at the beginning of the twenty-first century, no.22 ran in a paint scheme similar to that applied to Isle of Man Transport buses.

No	Builder	Year	Type	Seats	Status/Disposal
1	Milnes	1893	Unvestibuled saloon	36	MER
2	Milnes	1893	Unvestibuled saloon	36	MER
3	Milnes	1893	Unvestibuled saloon	36	Destroyed 1930 (a)
4	Milnes	1894	Vestibuled saloon	34	Destroyed 1930 (a)
5	Milnes	1894	Vestibuled saloon	32	MER
6	Milnes	1894	Vestibuled saloon	34	MER
7	Milnes	1894	Vestibuled saloon	34	MER
8	Milnes	1894	Vestibuled saloon	34	Destroyed 1930 (a)
9	Milnes	1894	Vestibuled saloon	34	MER
10	Milnes	1895	Vestibuled saloon	46	Converted to freight car (b)
11	Milnes	1895	Vestibuled saloon	46	Converted to freight car (b)
12	Milnes	1895	Vestibuled saloon	46	Converted to cattle car (b)
13	Milnes	1895	Vestibuled saloon	46	Converted to freight car (b)
14	Milnes	1898	Cross bench open	56	MER
15	Milnes	1898	Cross bench open	56	MER
16	Milnes	1898	Cross bench open	56	MER
17	Milnes	1898	Cross bench open	56	MER
18	Milnes	1898	Cross bench open	56	MER
19	Milnes	1899	Winter saloon	48	MER
20	Milnes	1899	Winter saloon	48	MER
21	Milnes	1899	Winter saloon	48	MER
22	Milnes	1899	Winter saloon	48	Body destroyed 1990 (c)
22	McArds	1992	Winter saloon	48	MER
23	IoMT&EPCo	1900	Locomotive	-	MER (d)
24	Milnes	1898	Cross bench open	56	Destroyed 1930 (a) (e)
25	Milnes	1898	Cross bench open	56	MER (e)
26	Milnes	1898	Cross bench open	56	MER (e)
27	Milnes	1898	Cross bench open	56	MER (e)
28	ER&TCW	1904	Cross bench open	56	MER
29	ER&TCW	1904	Cross bench open	56	MER
30	ER&TCW	1904	Cross bench open	56	MER
31	ER&TCW	1904	Cross bench open	56	MER
32	UEC	1906	Cross bench open	56	MER
33	UEC	1906	Cross bench open	56	MER
34	IoMR	1995	Locomotive	-	MER (f)

Notes:

(a)   Destroyed by fire at Laxey car shed 5th April 1930
(b)   Taken out of service 1902/03 and later converted to freight/cattle cars. No.10 now privately owned, nos 11 to 13 scrapped by 1950s
(c)   Body destroyed by fire at Derby Castle 30th September 1990
(d)   Rebuilt 1925 – now privately owned.
(e)   Previously trailers nos 40 to 43, converted to power cars 1903
(f)   Replica Snaefell Mountain Railway no.7 'Maria', regauged from 3ft 6in and fitted with diesel engine 2008

Builders:

ER&TCW	Electric Railway & Tramway Carriage Works Ltd, Preston
IoMR	Isle of Man Railway, Douglas
IoMT&EPCo	Isle of Man Tramways & Electric Power Co Ltd, Derby Castle
McArds	McArds Ltd, Port Erin, Isle of Man
Milnes	G.F.Milnes & Co Ltd, Birkenhead
UEC	United Electric Car Co Ltd, Preston

1. Douglas Horse Tramway

Horses have been trotting along Douglas Promenade hauling tramcars since 1876. Its popularity, and the intensity of service once provided, can be gauged by the fact that no less than 37 cars were purchased from a variety of sources between 1876 and 1896. A further 14 cars were imported by Douglas Corporation after they had taken over in 1901, the last in 1935. Amazingly, while the rest of such tramways have fallen by the wayside, horses continue to have right of way along the promenade hauling their vintage cars, although normally they can only be seen during the summer months. However, additionally a Santa service was operated on three days in December 2009.

DOUGLAS PROMENADE

1.   Presided over by the Jubilee Clock at the junction of Victoria Street and Loch Promenade, a horse stands ready to make the 1½-mile journey to Derby Castle shortly after midday on 11th June 1958. Toastrack no.21, built by G.F.Milnes of Birkenhead, started life in 1890 with eight benches for 32 passengers. In 1936 it was rebuilt with ten benches enabling 40 people to be carried, although with not quite as much leg-room. The clock was erected in 1887 to mark Queen Victoria's Golden Jubilee. While the clock still stands, this area of Douglas has seen considerable redevelopment in recent years. (R.E.Gee)

2.   Cyril trots along the Harris Promenade by the Gaiety Theatre heading towards the Sea Terminal with Milnes-built car no.37 of 1896 vintage in tow on 9th September 2006. The seating capacity of no.37 remains at 32 as originally intended. Easily read, even from this distance, above the car across Douglas Bay, is the large sign 'Electric Railway' which overlooks Derby Castle car sheds. The horse tram and electric railway joint termini at Derby Castle can be identified between the two lampposts on the left. Much nearer the camera, on the far left of the photograph, is the 50ft high Douglas War Memorial. (T.Heavyside)

3.   Horses are exchanged regularly on Queen's Promenade near the entrance to the stables, not far from Derby Castle. On the same sunny morning as the previous picture, Annif is about to start a spell of duty, its mate having gone off for a well-earned rest. (T.Heavyside)

2. Derby Castle to Groudle

DERBY CASTLE

IV. Track plan showing the close relationship between
the MER and the Douglas Horse Tramway.

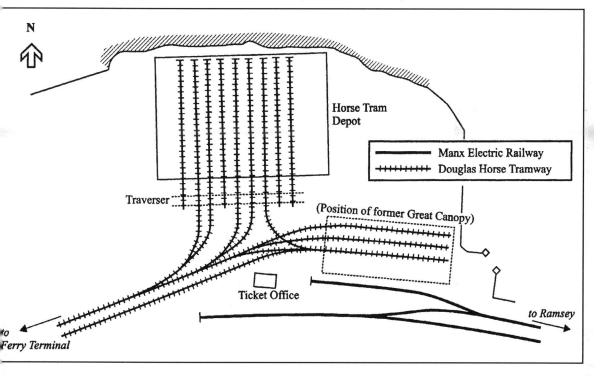

N

Horse Tram
Depot

———————— Manx Electric Railway
++++++++++ Douglas Horse Tramway

Traverser

(Position of former Great Canopy)

Ticket Office

to
Ferry Terminal

to Ramsey

4. A commercial postcard from about 1920. The promenade is bustling as a crowd of people make their way towards their lodgings after returning from a trip on the MER, while others simply take time out to enjoy the sunshine on this cloudless afternoon. The 'Great Canopy' dominates the scene on the left. No.39 was a 44-seater open cross bench trailer built by Milnes in 1894. It was one of those that perished in the fire at Laxey in April 1930. (J.D.Darby collection)

→ 5. The intricate ironwork of the 'Great Canopy' as built in 1896 can be studied in this photograph from 29th May 1939. This superb structure, 82ft long, 35ft wide, 18ft high to the eaves and 29ft to the apex, covered the terminal tracks of the horse tramway. Part of the 13ft high clock tower can be seen above the gables. Stabled under cover, awaiting four-legged power, are three double-decked horse cars and toastrack no.25. Advertisements for Jacob's biscuits and Guinness are prominent. The canopy had been the responsibility of Douglas Corporation since 1901, when they took over the horse tramway. To the left of 'Winter Saloon' no.21 are the imposing towers guarding the entrance to Derby Castle hotel and entertainment complex, the main buildings of which can be seen on the right-hand side of the picture. (D.J.Mitchell collection)

→ 6. Douglas Corporation purchased Derby Castle in 1963 and subsequently set about its demolition, revealing the southern boundary walls and buildings of the car sheds. No.32 drifts towards the terminus on 29th May 1967. (D.J.Mitchell)

7.   Mail was transported between Derby Castle and Laxey from 1894, and to and from Ramsey once the line had been completed in 1899. Uniquely, from 1903, the conductors on a couple of southbound services were authorized to collect the contents from eight lineside postboxes, some having been repositioned on railway-owned land. Before MER employees were allowed to have charge of the keys, they had to be specially sworn in by the GPO. Here in May 1969, a time when the replacement Summerland leisure centre was still under construction on the old Derby Castle site, sacks of mail are being loaded into van no.13 ready for onward transmission to Ramsey. The van was shipped over from Milnes factory in Birkenhead in 1904 and could carry up to 5 tons. A reduced winter service from September 1972 meant it was only practicable to continue to collect items from the three postboxes located to the north of Laxey. The contract finally ended when MER services were suspended on 30th September 1975. (D.J.Mitchell)

➜ 8.   Early one morning in July 1973 no.6 sets out for the north while nos 21 and 27 will follow later. A rather plain, hipped roof on the 'Great Canopy' now provided protection for the horse trams. The former entrance area to Derby Castle had been resurfaced for car parking. (D.J.Mitchell)

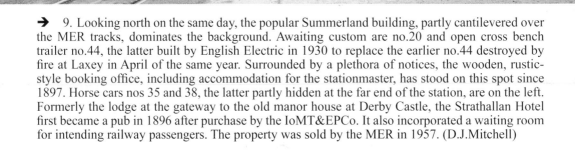

➜ 9. Looking north on the same day, the popular Summerland building, partly cantilevered over the MER tracks, dominates the background. Awaiting custom are no.20 and open cross bench trailer no.44, the latter built by English Electric in 1930 to replace the earlier no.44 destroyed by fire at Laxey in April of the same year. Surrounded by a plethora of notices, the wooden, rustic-style booking office, including accommodation for the stationmaster, has stood on this spot since 1897. Horse cars nos 35 and 38, the latter partly hidden at the far end of the station, are on the left. Formerly the lodge at the gateway to the old manor house at Derby Castle, the Strathallan Hotel first became a pub in 1896 after purchase by the IoMT&EPCo. It also incorporated a waiting room for intending railway passengers. The property was sold by the MER in 1957. (D.J.Mitchell)

10.   The month after the previous two pictures were taken, Summerland suffered a disastrous fire, tragically involving loss of life. In September of the following year some of the resultant exposed girders can be seen as 'Tunnel Car' no.9 and an attached trailer, paced by a Manx-registered Jaguar, approach the terminus. The doorway on the left was the access point to an underground discotheque. The entrance to the car sheds is visible behind the trailer, as is the Douglas Bay Hotel at Port Jack to the right of the sign for the Park Stadium. (D.J.Mitchell)

→   11. A highlight of many gala events in recent years has been an early morning parade of stock, as on 21st August 1998. Nos 26, 2 and 16 are identifiable. The Summerland family entertainment centre and Aquadrome again form the backdrop, although the footbridge seen in picture 7 that provided an emergency exit to the promenade was no longer available for patrons or, indeed, photographers. (T.Heavyside)

→   12. Decorated with some 1,600 coloured lights and illuminated roof boards to commemorate 125 years of steam working on the island, no.9 proudly poses for the camera on 21st August 1998. Note, too, the island insignia, three conjoined armoured legs. This 'Tunnel Car' has often been employed on the midweek evening shuttle services to Groudle when, especially after nightfall, it makes a splendid sight. Regrettably the 'Great Canopy' was dismantled in 1980 after being deemed unsafe, and all that remains as a reminder of the structure are the bases of the sawn-off stanchions, one of which is to the right of no.9. Overlooking the scene, above the horse tram depot, are the offices of Isle of Man Transport. In 2000, staff were relocated to a new building by the steam railway terminus in Douglas (see *Douglas to Peel* picture 21). (T.Heavyside)

13.   In 1996 former Lisbon Tramways no.360, a 40-seater saloon with four 25hp motors built by John Stephenson Car Company of New York, was imported from Portugal with a view to the possible reuse of its bogies. In 2000 the maroon-painted body was stood on wooden sleepers in the 'Groudle Siding' (so-called as one-time it was often used by cars on the Groudle service) as a waiting area, although obviously on this occasion people preferred the benches outside. Covered protection for passengers had been a continuing problem ever since the demolition of the 'Great Canopy' in 1980, an old Leyland National bus and service cars fulfilling the role in other years. The Strathallan Hotel has been renamed Terminus Tavern. After a number of years out of public view, the body of no.360 was moved to a farm near St John's in December 2009 for use as a seating area during equestrian events. Its present setting is a far cry indeed from its birthplace on the other side of the Atlantic or the busy streets of Lisbon, where it spent almost 90 years before moving to the island. (D.Robinson)

14.   A permanent solution to the lack of covered waiting facilities was resolved by the erection of the basic shelter seen here on the left. Nos 21 and 44 will form the 10.40 to Ramsey on 9th September 2006. In preparation the trolley pole has still to be turned round. Note the ancient symbol of the island, the Three Legs of Man, suspended from the arches of the street lamps. (T.Heavyside)

DERBY CASTLE CAR SHEDS

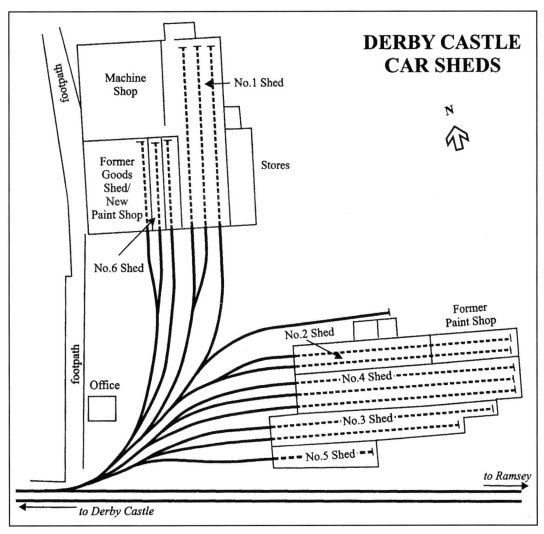

DERBY CASTLE CAR SHEDS

Machine Shop

No.1 Shed

Stores

N

Former Goods Shed/ New Paint Shop

No.6 Shed

footpath

footpath

Office

Former Paint Shop

No.2 Shed

No.4 Shed

No.3 Shed

No.5 Shed

to Ramsey

to Derby Castle

V. Track plan of the depot before redevelopment.

← 15. Entry to the depot can only be gained off the northbound track. Cars going on duty thus have to travel 'wrong line' to the station. With the broad sweep of Douglas Bay in the background, no.33 clatters over the points on its way towards Ramsey in July 1967. The conductor checks the tickets while moving along the footboard - a once regular practice but now frowned upon. No.33 was the last power car purchased by the MER in 1906. Notice the three-way point, from which access is gained to the various sheds, in the centre foreground. (J.Fozard collection)

← 16. The depot was created in 1893 on land reclaimed from the former Port-e-Vada creek, a veritable hotchpotch of buildings subsequently springing up across the site. Here, in a picture believed to date from 1904, the 20ft 6in long no.23 rests on borrowed bogies outside no.1 shed. In accordance with a one-time statutory requirement, in addition to the electric headlight, an oil lamp is displayed on the bonnet. Note the MER lettering on the side of the cab. (B.C.Lane collection)

17. Cross bench open trailer no.50 sits under the arched roof of no.1 shed on a pleasant day in August 1963. The structure on the left-hand side, where the boiler house originally stood, served as the goods shed from 1908 to 1966, and then as a store until it became the paint shop in 1989. Behind the men attending to the motor car is the 1924-built no.6 shed, this now being used as the joiners' shop. The staff mess hut is on the right. (J.L.Stevenson)

18.   The three tracks inside the 112ft-long no.1 shed, known as the 'Hospital Roads' since this is where most of the repair and heavy maintenance work is undertaken, were occupied by nos 22 (burnt out 25 years later), 1 and 'Ratchet Car' 31 when visited in May 1965. Upturned wooden troughs protect the overhead wires. (D.J.Mitchell)

→ 19. The ridge-roofed nos 2, 4 and 3 sheds (most peculiarly the centre shed was identified as no.4) were erected during the years 1894 to 1896. The lean-to no.5 shed on the right was added in 1924. Visible on 14th June 1958 are nos 5, 7, 43, 33 and 25. Very little of the decorative woodwork that had once adorned the gables of nos 2 and 4 sheds remained in place at this time. (J.L.Stevenson)

→   20. Nos 2 and 30, together with a number of other vehicles, are protected from the vagaries of the weather inside no.2 shed during May 1965. The pits allow easy access for maintenance purposes. (D.J.Mitchell)

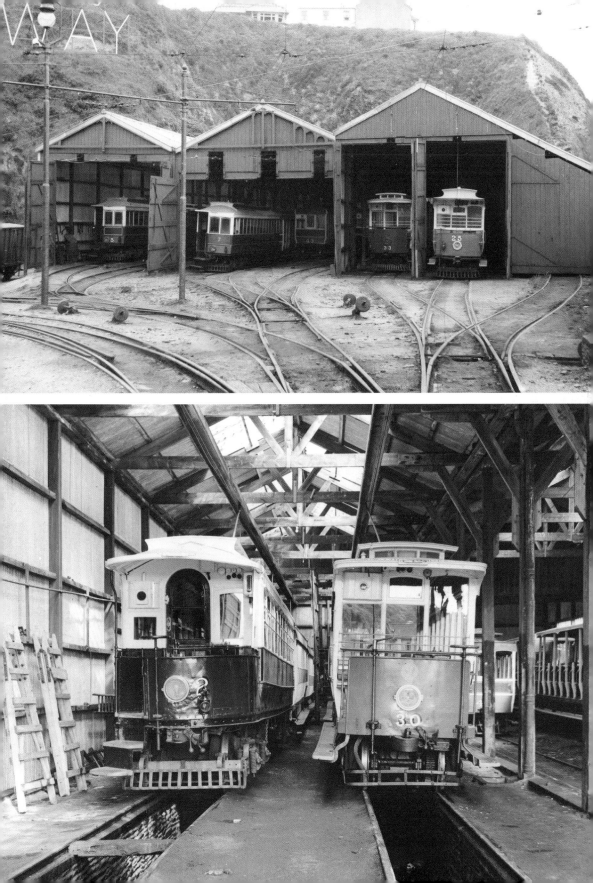

21.   The track layout can be studied in detail in this bird's-eye view from 4th June 1968. Lower right 'Tunnel Car' no.6 rests outside no.1 shed with nos 2, 4, 3 and 5 sheds to its left. Three vans, nos 11 and 14 are identifiable, occupy what was referred to as the 'Bonner Siding' (once used by the short-lived Bonner road-rail vehicles) by the north elevation of no.2 shed. Next to no.11 a bogie from beneath a passenger car can also be discerned. Near the entrance is the yard master's hut. (D.J.Mitchell)

→ 22. With no.1 shed in the background, no.6 slowly makes its way towards the exit on 21st August 1998. This shed was re-roofed eight years earlier in 1990, with the MER wooden mascot, 'Tommy Milner', being restored to its rightful place at the apex on completion. According to legend, as long as 'Tommy' stays in position the MER will remain open for business. (T.Heavyside)

↓ 23. A new building with a single ridge roof replaced nos 2 to 5 sheds in 1997. At the same time the track layout was completely remodelled, but in practice this proved far from satisfactory and was torn up and redesigned in 2001. The relaid fan radiating from the entry point was recorded on 8th August 2002. Portable levers are used to change the points. The body of no.22, on the left, was constructed on the island by McArds of Port Erin, after the original 1899 body (see picture 18) had been destroyed by fire at the depot in September 1990. No.22 is in a red and cream livery similar to the Isle of Man Transport bus fleet. More vehicles rest within the confines of the shed. In 2003 more traditional wooden hinged doors were hung in place of the metal concertina variety seen here. (T.Heavyside)

PORT JACK

24.   With the Douglas Bay Hotel dominating this Edwardian scene, a power car and trailer, with a full compliment of passengers, climbs the steep incline towards Onchan Head, while others prefer to stroll on this pleasant afternoon. The hotel was devastated by fire in 1988. Business premises now grace the site. (A.D.Packer collection)

➔ 25. No.15 drifts downgrade past the distinctive row of balconied shops en route to Derby Castle in September 1956. The motorman appears to be the sole occupant. (J.Fozard collection)

➔   26. On a glorious July morning in 1973, no.9 grinds its way round the tight curve on its way north with another well-laden service. In the middle distance is Douglas Bay and Promenade. (D.J.Mitchell)

Derby Castle to Ramsey	1937	1938
Passengers carried	500,372	456,679
Passenger mileage	291,201	282,409
Passenger receipts	£24,024	£21,682
Goods tonnage	11,064	7,039
Goods mileage	25,597	18,381
Goods receipts	£3,201	£2,864
Livestock mileage	69	72
Livestock receipts	£3	£4
Note: Totals relate to year ending 30th September		

ONCHAN HEAD

27.   The shelter, dating from 1899, was clearly showing its age, as was the former booking office, displaying a MER timetable, when photographed on 4th July 1975. This was once a very busy station with its own stationmaster, much business being generated by visitors to the nearby White City leisure park and fun fair. The station buildings were demolished in 1978 and the last of the White City rides and sideshows closed at the end of the 1985 summer season. (J.L.Stevenson)

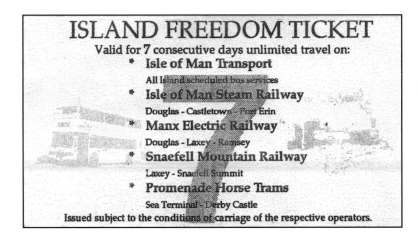

ISLAND FREEDOM TICKET
Valid for 7 consecutive days unlimited travel on:
*   **Isle of Man Transport**
    All Island scheduled bus services
*   **Isle of Man Steam Railway**
    Douglas - Castletown - Port Erin
*   **Manx Electric Railway**
    Douglas - Laxey - Ramsey
*   **Snaefell Mountain Railway**
    Laxey - Snaefell Summit
*   **Promenade Horse Trams**
    Sea Terminal - Derby Castle
Issued subject to the conditions of carriage of the respective operators.

28.   The area looked much smarter when observed on 8th August 2002 as nos 9 and 62 headed towards Douglas, the replacement shelter serving the needs of both bus and rail passengers, although the seat was clearly marked 'Manx Electric Railway'. The light bulbs remain attached but not the other embellishments seen on no.9 in picture 12. Other than the three replacement trailers received after the Laxey fire in 1930, no.62 was the last trailer to enter service back in 1906. (T.Heavyside)

HOWSTRAKE

29.　　Running parallel with the A11 road, no.19 turns inland and begins the 1-in-24 descent towards Groudle on 8th August 2002. The roof parapet on the three-arch stone shelter, provided by the owners of an adjacent holiday camp about 1910, looks to be in need of some attention. This is an isolated spot and the shelter has been hardly used since the camp closed in 1973. (T.Heavyside)

MONDAY, 28th JUNE 1937, and until further notice.

The Snaefell Mountain Railway & Motor Char-a-Banc Service between Snaefell Bungalow Station and the Manx Switzerland, Tholt-e-Will, Sulby Glen, now open.　　Cars as required by traffic.

PASSENGERS CHANGE AT LAXEY FOR THE GLORIOUS TRIP TO THE SUMMIT OF SNAEFELL MOUNTAIN (2,034 FEET ABOVE SEA LEVEL).

From Douglas.　The run on the Open Cars by the Royal Mail & Coast Route to Ramsey through magnificent Woodland & Marine Scenery is of unrivalled popularity.

DOUGLAS (DERBY CASTLE)	Sundays ...dep.	7 0			10 0			11 0	12 0	1 0	2 0	2 30	3 0	3 30	4 0	4 30		6 30		8 0	9 0		10 30		
	Weekdays dep.	7 0	9 0	10 0	10 30	11 0	12 0	1 0	2 0	2 30	3 0	3 30	4 0	4 30	5 30	6 30	7 15	8 0	9 0	10 0			11 0
GROUDLE GLEN	,,	a.m.				noon	p.m.			A					Boat Car	Mall Car				From Laxey	
BALDRINE	,,	Boat Car								Mall & Boat												
GARWICK GLEN	,,									Car												
LAXEY (Change for Snaefell Mountain Summit & Sulby Glen)	Sundays .. dep.	7 30			10 30			11 30	12 30	1 30	2 30	3 0	3 30	3 50	4 30	5 0		7 0		8 30	9 30		11 0	11 15	
	Weekdays dep.	7 30	9 25	10 30	11 0	11 30	12 30	1 30	2 30	3 0	3 30	3 50	4 30	5 0	6 0	7 0	7 45	8 30	9 30	10 30			11 30
DHOON GLEN	,,																				
GLEN MONA	,,																				
BALLAGLASS GLEN	,,																				
BALLAJORA LEWAIGUE	,,																				
	Sundays ...arr.	8 10			11 15			12 15	1 15	2 15	3 15	3 45	4 15	4 25	5 15	5 45		7 40		9 10	10 10		11 40	11 50	
RAMSEY (PLAZA)	Weekdays arr.	8 10	10 5	11 15	11 45	12 15	1 15	2 15	3 15	3 45	4 15	4 25	5 15	5 45	6 45	7 40	8 25	9 10	10 10	11 10			12 10

From Ramsey　ALL THE CHARMING GLENS EN ROUTE ARE IN MAGNIFICENT FOLIAGE.

RAMSEY (PLAZA)	Sundays ...dep.			8 30		10 30	11 30	12 15	1 30	2 0	2 30	3 15	4 0	4 30	5 0	5 45	6 30			7 45	9 15		10 30	
	Weekdays dep.	6 45		8 30	9 30	10 30	11 30	12 15	1 30	2 0	2 30	3 15	4 0	4 30	5 0	5 45	6 30	7 15	7 45	9 15	9 45	10 30
LEWAIGUE BALLAJORA	,,	a.m.				a.m.	p.m.												Boat Car	
BALLAGLASS GLEN	,,	B								Mall and										
GLEN MONA	,,	Mall &								Boat Cars										
DHOON GLEN	,,	Boat Car																	
LAXEY (Change for Snaefell Mountain Summit & Sulby Glen)	Sundays ...dep.			9 10		11 15	12 15	1 0	2 15	2 40	3 15	4 0	4 45	5 15	5 45	6 30	7 15		8 25	9 55		11 10	
	Weekdays dep.	7 30	8 15	9 10	10 10	11 15	12 15	1 0	2 15	2 40	3 15	4 0	4 45	5 15	5 45	6 30	7 15	8 0	8 25	9 55	10 25	11 10 Stop
GARWICK GLEN	,,																			
BALDRINE	,,																			
GROUDLE GLEN	,,																			
DOUGLAS (DERBY CASTLE)	Sundays ...arr.			9 40		11 45	12 45	1 30	2 45	3 10	3 45	4 30	5 15	5 45	6 15	7 0	7 45		8 55	10 25		
	Weekdays arr.	8 0	8 45	9 40	10 40	11 45	12 45	1 30	2 45	3 10	3 45	4 30	5 15	5 45	6 15	7 0	7 45	8 30	8 55	10 25	10 55	

Special Note : A—Mail Express, stops en route on Weekdays at Baldrine and Laxey only ; B—In connection with 8.30 & 9 a.m. Steamers from Douglas. Sunday Service shewn in Red

GROUDLE

30.   This postcard was posted by a visitor to an address in Belfast on 10th August 1909 and may even have started its journey to Ireland on board a MER car. It depicts passengers from Douglas walking in the direction of the 1893-opened hotel. (T.Heavyside collection)

31.   No.6 and English Electric 1930-built trailer no.40 have just negotiated the near 180 degree curve in front of the old toll house and are slowing for the mandatory stop as they arrive from the north on 23rd July 1960. The house remained standing until 1988 although tolls had not been collected from road travellers since the 1920s. (J.L.Stevenson)

32.   Trailer no.47, constructed by Milnes in 1899 with 44 seats and complete with a clerestory roof, brings up the rear of a Laxey-bound service in July 1966. The castellated parapet of the three-span viaduct that carries both road and rails over Lhen Coan is in sight of the motorman. To the right of the hotel is the ornate gateway to the glen itself. (J.Fozard collection)

33.   The centenary plaque was unveiled on 7th September 1993. The lever below switches the crossover points, this seeing frequent use in the days when passenger levels were such that at peak times a shuttle service had to be provided between here and Derby Castle. (T.Heavyside)

34.　　Four teenagers accompanied by a younger child on their way to Douglas prepare to board either no.6 or trailer no.47 on 8th August 2002. The shelter dates from 1894. The centenary plaque can be seen to the left of no.6. (T.Heavyside)

35.　　A minute or so later nos 6 and 47 resume their journey south. A much more modest sign compared to that seen in picture 32 marks the entrance to the glen, now one of seventeen Manx National Glens maintained by the Forestry Department. (T.Heavyside)

3. Groudle Glen Railway

Visitors were first allowed to roam this enchanting glen in August 1893. Over the ensuing years a number of attractions were developed, including a ¾-mile 2ft 0in gauge railway, opened in May 1896, that can proudly boast to run uphill to the sea. It lay dormant during World War I, and then again throughout the 1940s before services resumed in 1950, although only as far as the Headland. No trains ran during 1959 or 1960 and while steam was again to be seen in 1961 and 1962, it failed to reopen for the 1963 summer season and the track was later lifted as far as the Headland and the stock dispersed. Undoubtedly this would have been the end of the story had members of the Isle of Man Steam Railway Supporters' Association not intervened during the early 1980s. Under their stewardship a short section was revived in time for Christmas 1983, since when the railway has gone from strength to strength, trains returning to the original terminus at Sea Lion Rocks, after an absence of over 50 years, in May 1992. In 2010, in addition to Easter and Christmas, trains ran every Sunday during the summer months, as well as some Saturdays and Wednesday evenings in high season.

Locomotives 2010

Name	Type	Builder	Year
Sea Lion	2-4-0T	Bagnall	1896 (a)
Parracombe	0-4-0DM	Baguley	1947
Dolphin	4wDM	Hunslet	1952
Walrus	4wDM	Hunslet	1952
Polar Bear	4wBE	Wingrove & Rogers	1988 (b)
Annie	0-4-2T	Booth	1997

Notes:
(a) Rebuilt British Nuclear Fuels, Sellafield 1987
(b) Rebuilt Alan Keef Ltd, Ross-on-Wye 2004

Builders:

Bagnall	W.G.Bagnall Ltd, Stafford
Baguley	E.E.Baguley Ltd, Burton-upon-Trent
Booth	R.Booth, Isle of Man
Hunslet	Hunslet Engine Co Ltd, Leeds
Wingrove & Rogers	Wingrove & Rogers Ltd, Liverpool

↗ 36. The sylvan setting viewed on 25th May 1958. The vast majority of passengers approach by way of the path to the right of the one on which the photographer is standing, after following a zigzag course through the glen from the roadside entrance to be seen in pictures 32 and 35. Three of the original four-wheeled coaches, each designed to carry ten people, shelter under the station roof. They were all 13ft 0in long, 3ft 2in wide and 6ft 7in high. No.3, nearest the entrance, arrived from G.F.Milnes in time for the opening in 1896. The coach on the left looks as if it needs to be put back on the rails. (C.Gammell/H.Davies collection)

➜   37. A rejuvenated *Sea Lion* stands outside the reconstructed station building, finished in 1993, on 20th July 1996. This was the year the railway celebrated its centenary. Compare this view of the engine with its derelict condition at the Kirk Michael Steam Centre in September 1968 as portrayed in *Douglas to Ramsey* picture 82. It was moved to Loughborough in 1981 before returning to the island two years later. (T.Heavyside)

LHEN COAN

38.   A second 2-4-0T, *Polar Bear*, was acquired from Bagnall's in 1905, works no.1781. It has slightly larger dimensions than *Sea Lion*, and hence a little more powerful. After the abandonment of the line by its former operators *Polar Bear* left the island in 1967 and is now normally resident at the Amberley Museum near Arundel, West Sussex. It revisited its old haunts in 1996, as it has on a couple of other occasions, and is seen at rest outside the three-road engine shed on 20th July. The plaque below the apex is dated 1986. The original shed had just a single road. (T.Heavyside)

39.   There were other visitors in 1998 as part of the 125th anniversary celebrations of the Isle of Man Railway, services over the section from Douglas to Peel having been inaugurated in July 1873. Centenarian, ex-Dinorwic Quarry Hunslet 0-4-0ST *Jonathan* (named *Bernstein* in its pre-preservation days) was shipped across from the West Lancashire Light Railway at Hesketh Bank, near Preston, as was fellow 0-4-0ST *Peter Pan*, built by Kerr Stuart in 1922, from the Leighton Buzzard Narrow Gauge Railway. They pose outside the shed on 22nd August 1998. (T.Heavyside).

40.   A non-operating day in September 2009 allows an unimpeded view of the current layout. The two-road shed was completed in 2008, the former engine shed beyond now being used to provide covered accommodation for the carriages. (T.Heavyside)

HEADLAND

41.   Having just passed Lime Kiln Halt, diesel-mechanical *Dolphin* enters the passing loop with a demonstration freight on 17th July 1996. *Dolphin* and its twin *Walrus* were imported in 1983 after previous employment on a pleasure railway at Dodington House, near Chipping Sodbury, north of Bath, and before that for various industrial concerns. Normally access to the railway can only be gained on foot by way of some steep, narrow, winding footpaths, so larger items, including locomotives, have to be carted in across the fields to the right of the picture by agreement with the local farmer. (T.Heavyside)

↗ 42. The dramatic coastal scenery is seen to good effect as *Sea Lion*, with 0-4-2T *Annie* trailing at the rear, makes its way towards Sea Lion Rocks at the head of a Wednesday evening service on 7th August 2002. *Annie* was built by Groudle-volunteer Richard Booth to the same dimensions as a 2ft 6in gauge engine (apart from the necessary alterations to accommodate the narrower width between the rails) exported by Bagnall's to the Gentle Annie Tramway, Gisborne, New Zealand, in 1911. When trains returned to this stretch in 1992, for safety reasons the rails had to be moved a few feet inland. The old formation can be seen to the left of *Sea Lion*. On the skyline, above the leading coaches, MER traction poles can be observed near Howstrake. (T.Heavyside)

→ 43. In 1921 Wingrove & Rogers, then of Southport, supplied two centre-cab 4-wheeled battery-electric locomotives, although for extra stability pony trucks were soon added at each end. Like their steam counterparts they were also named *Sea Lion* and *Polar Bear*. With the old station buildings on the right, staff and passengers pose for the photographer before *Polar Bear* makes its way back to Lhen Coan, sometime during the 1920s. Both battery-electrics have long since been scrapped, but a replica of *Polar Bear*, fashioned by Alan Keef in 2004 from a later product of Wingrove & Rogers, is now resident in the glen.
(Isle of Man Steam Railway
Supporters' Association collection)

NORTH OF HEADLAND

SEA LION ROCKS

44.   *Annie* and *Sea Lion* pause for a few minutes at the terminus on 7th August 2002. The current station building was made available to passengers the same year. However it is now over 70 years since sea lions were kept in the small cove beyond the stop blocks, as were two polar bears at one time. An aviary has also long since disappeared. (T.Heavyside)

4. Halfway House to Laxey

HALFWAY HOUSE

45.   Returning to the route of the MER, this request stop, 3½ miles into our journey, where the A11 joins the main A2 road from Douglas to the north, is more or less equidistant between Derby Castle and Laxey. No.20 crosses the A11 on its way to the capital on 4th July 1975, while the A2 can be glimpsed on the left. The postbox is still extant although it is now nearly 40 years since it was last emptied by a conductor of a passing MER train. (J.L.Stevenson)

BALDRINE

46.   In this northward view from July 1975 the shelter, erected in 1899, appears in a state of disrepair. (J.L.Stevenson)

47.   Having been called out to attend to some repairs needed to the overhead wiring, no.7, towing a tower wagon, scurries by in the direction of Laxey on 8th August 2002. The shelter looked a good deal smarter after some much-needed renovation work carried out during the early 1990s. The postbox remains a feature. (T.Heavyside)

GARWICK GLEN

48.   No.5 halts on its way north on 18th May 1959. In days gone by thousands of day-trippers were attracted to the glen (once managed by the MER) each year, extra cars often being needed to return the throngs to Douglas, a stationmaster being in attendance to supervise. As well as providing a pleasant route down to the beach, the sign above the entrance advises there were also smugglers' caves and a maze to be explored, with a tearoom and a fully licensed hotel available. On return passengers could check their weight, to their joy or disbelief, for the sum of one penny on the scales under the commodious shelter. The glen passed into private hands in the late 1960s, since when the public has only rarely been allowed access. The kiosk on the left was demolished in 1968 and the by-then decaying shelter in 1979. The halt sees little custom these days. (A.D.Packer)

BALLABEG

49.   Here we are looking downhill in the direction of Laxey on 1st July 1975. Local residents have been able to take advantage of this corrugated iron shelter since 1905. Behind the traction pole is one of 34 feeder pillars provided along the route for the overhead. The button attached to the pole nearer the camera is used to extinguish the flashing red lights at the nearby level crossing (behind the photographer) when single line running is in operation using the right-hand track. The activation and cancellation of the crossing lights that warn road users and allow MER cars precedence is normally controlled by treadles, but when running 'wrong-line' towards Laxey the motorman must halt before the crossing, reach out and depress a button to activate the lights. He then has to stop a second time by this post so as to allow road traffic to flow freely again. (J.L.Stevenson)

FAIRY COTTAGE

50.   Overlooked by the houses at a slightly higher level in the background, the sharp curve to the south of the station is apparent in this photograph taken on 4th September 1982. The shelter was subsequently rebuilt in 1992. Note, too, the crossover. (J.L.Stevenson)

51.   The doyen of the 2-4-0Ts built for the Isle of Man Railway by Beyer Peacock of Manchester in 1873, no.1 *Sutherland*, was a most unusual visitor on 21st August 1998. It had just laboured 'wrong line' up the steep incline (1-in-25 in places) from Laxey hauling trailer no.58 as part of the celebrations to mark the 125th anniversary of the IoMR. (T.Heavyside)

← 52. Passengers aboard no.1 and an attached trailer enjoy the visual delights of the coastline as they cautiously continue the long descent towards Laxey on Monday 29th May 1967. The walls of Laxey Harbour can be espied down below. Travellers are advised to 'Alight here for Laxey Beach'. (D.J.Mitchell)

↙ 53. A few minutes later on this crystal clear day, the photographer recorded 'Paddlebox' no.25 (note the raised footboard over the Brush bogies) and a trailer passing southbound. The gentleman privileged to accompany the motorman no doubt felt this a perfect way to spend a Bank Holiday afternoon. Beyond the dormer bungalow on the right, less than half-a-mile away as the crow flies, the route of the MER can be traced as it climbs along the other side of the valley from Laxey towards Bulgham Bay. The white-painted house at a slightly higher level can also be seen in picture 84. (D.J.Mitchell)

LAXEY CAR SHED

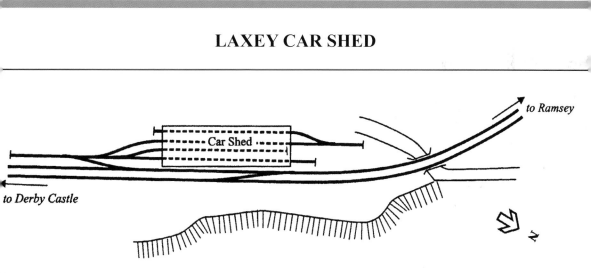

VI. Track plan of the depot before it was rebuilt in 2009.

Commencing FRIDAY, 17th September, 1937, and until further notice.															
FROM DOUGLAS						**WEEK DAYS**								**SUNDAYS**	
		a.m.	9 0	10 0	11 30	p.m. 1 0	2 30	3 30	4 30	5 30	6 30	9 5		11 0	p.m. 2 15	p.m. 7 15
DOUGLAS (DERBY CASTLE)	dep.	7 15							A					C		
GROUDLE GLEN	,,		Mail Car	Mail Car				Mail Car D					From Dhoon Quarry B			
BALDRINE	,,															
GARWICK GLEN	,,															
LAXEY	,,	7 40	9 30	10 30	12 0	1 30	3 0	3 55	5 0	6 0	7 0	9 35	9 10	11 30	2 45	7 45
DHOON	,,															
GLEN MONA, BALLAGLASS	,,															
RAMSEY (PLAZA) ...	arr.	8 25	10 10	11 10	12 40	2 10	3 40	4 30	5 40	6 40	7 40	10 15	9 35	12 10	3 20	8 20
FROM RAMSEY						**WEEK DAYS**									**SUNDAYS**	
RAMSEY (PLAZA)	dep.	a.m. 7 0		8 30	10 15	11 30	p.m. 1 0	2 10	4 10	5 10	6 45	7 45	8 45	9 45	10 30	3 30	8 30
GLEN MONA, BALLAGLASS ,,		Mail Car						Mail Car					B 9 10	C	To Laxey		
DHOON	,,		From Laxey										To Dhoon Quarry STOP			
LAXEY	,,	7 40	8 15	9 10	10 55	12 10	1 40	2 50	4 50	5 50	7 25	8 25		10 25	11 10 STOP	4 5	9 5
GARWICK GLEN	,,	For Liverpool Boat															
BALDRINE	,,															
GROUDLE GLEN	,,															
DOUGLAS (DERBY CASTLE)	arr.	8 10	8 45	9 40	11 25	12 40	2 10	3 15	5 20	6 20	7 55	8 55		10 55		4 35	9 35

Winter Fares: Douglas & Laxey, 1/- Return; Douglas & Ramsey, 2/2 Return; Laxey & Ramsey, 1/2 Return

A—Liable to delay awaiting arrival of Boat Passengers. B—Saturdays only. C—Thursdays and Saturdays only. D—Liable to delay awaiting arrival of Mails.

54.   The original shed was gutted by fire on the evening of Saturday 5th April 1930. Listed among the major items destroyed were power cars nos 3, 4, 8 and 24, trailers nos 34, 35, 38, 39, 40, 41 and 44, together with three tower wagons. Here no.19 hastens towards Douglas past the four-road, 150ft 6in-long replacement shed in May 1939. The first Laxey terminus, used in 1894 and 1895, was located just beyond the shed. The high ground in the background forms part of the Northern Upland Massif. (D.J.Mitchell collection)

55.   For many years the shed was used mainly as a store. Resting within the corrugated iron walls during August 1963 is former saloon car no.10, one of four constructed by Milnes in 1895. All four were taken out of passenger service in 1902/03, converted for the conveyance of freight or cattle and renumbered, no.10 becoming no.26. This is the only survivor of the quartet. It could carry up to 7 tons. On the right is no.17, a cross bench open car constructed by Milnes in 1898. (J.L.Stevenson)

56.　　During its short sojourn on the MER in 1998, *Sutherland* was housed at the depot, and is seen outside the south end ready to take centre stage as part of the ongoing IoMR 125 celebrations on 21st August. On the left is the chassis of trailer no.52, built by Milnes in 1893, the body having been removed in 1947. In its new guise it has been available for use by the permanent way department. The fourth road in the shed could only be accessed from the north end. (T.Heavyside)

COMMENCING MONDAY, 15th SEPTEMBER, 1969, AND UNTIL FURTHER NOTICE

Connecting Bus from Central Bus Station, Lord Street		8 35	9 35	11 35	1 5	2 35	4 5	5 35		8 35
FROM DOUGLAS				**WEEKDAYS**						
DOUGLAS (DERBY CASTLE) dep.	7 0	8 45	9 45	11 45	1 15	2 45	4 15	5 45	7 15	8 45
	a.m.				p.m.					
MAJESTIC HOTEL ,,										
GROUDLE GLEN ,,										
BALDRINE ,,										
GARWICK ,,										
LAXEY ,,	7 25	9 10	10 10	12 10	1 40	3 10	4 40	6 10	7 40	9 10
DHOON				p.m.						
GLEN MONA, BALLAGLASS ,,										
RAMSEY (PLAZA) arr.	8 10	9 55	10 55	12 55	2 25	3 55	5 25	6 55	8 25	9 55
FROM RAMSEY				**WEEKDAYS**						
RAMSEY (PLAZA) dep.	7 15	8 25	10 25	11 50	1 25	2 50	4 25	5 45	7 20	8 25
BALLAGLASS, GLEN MONA ,,					p.m.					
DHOON ,,										
LAXEY ,,	8 0	9 5	11 5	12 35	2 5	3 30	5 5	6 30	8 0	9 5
GARWICK ,,				p.m.						
BALDRINE ,,										
GROUDLE GLEN ,,										
MAJESTIC HOTEL ,,										
DOUGLAS (DERBY CASTLE) arr.	8 30	9 35	11 35	1 5	2 35	4 0	5 35	7 0	8 30	9 35
Connecting Bus to Victoria Pier & Central Bus Station, Lord Street	8 36	9 36	11 36	1 10	2 36	4 6	5 40	7 21		

Return Fares

DOUGLAS to:—

Groudle	1/2
Garwick	1/5
LAXEY	2/3
Dhoon	2/9
Glen Mona	3/-
Ballaglass	3/3
Ballajora	4/-
RAMSEY	4/6

RAMSEY to:—

Ballajora	10d
Ballaglass	1/5
Glen Mona	1/8
Dhoon	2/-
LAXEY	2/6
Fairy Cottage	2/9
Halfway House	3/3
DOUGLAS	4/6

Weekly Tickets and Contract Tickets available at Reduced Rates

57. No crew or passenger car has been based here since 1999. On 28th April 2001 no.21 glides past on its way north, while stored near the end of the headshunt is out-of-use 6-ton open wagon no.8, a product of Milnes in 1897/98. In 2002 the building was declared unsafe, all the resident stock transferred elsewhere and the roof removed, although for convenience on occasions no.7 has been stabled here when in use as a works car. (T.Heavyside)

58 During 2009 the shed was rebuilt to a similar design as the previous building, although there are now only three roads inside, the most westerly track having been lifted. It provides a secure storage facility. The north and east walls were recorded on 24th September 2009. The remains of wagon no.8 stand on the short length of protruding track. (T.Heavyside)

GLEN ROY VIADUCT

59.   On special occasions in 1998, IoMR 2-4-0T no.1 *Sutherland* of 1873 vintage ran side by side with MER no.1 of 1893 between Laxey and Fairy Cottage. Here on 21st August they accelerate away from the lofty four-arch viaduct, the north end being visible on the right-hand side of the photograph. Douglas & Laxey Coast Electric Tramway has been inscribed along the lower panel of MER no.1 as per ownership in 1893. As clearly indicated by the sign on the traction pole speed must not exceed 5mph while crossing the bridge. Trains terminated at this spot in 1896, pending completion of the viaduct in 1898. (T.Heavyside)

TIME TABLE—Saturday, 29th May, 1965 and until 17th September, 1965

Time from Derby Castle :—   THE SNAEFELL MOUNTAIN RAILWAY OPEN from 15th May until 30th September, 1965   CARS AS REQUIRED BY TRAFFIC.
Groudle 12 mins.; Garwick 20 mins.; Dhoon 45 mins.; Ballaglass 55 mins. Change at Laxey for the Glorious Trip to the Summit of Snaefell Mountain (2,034 feet above sea level). The run on the Open Cars by the Direct Coast Route to Ramsey through magnificent Woodland and Marine Scenery is of unrivalled popularity.

FROM DOUGLAS   WEEKDAYS   SUNDAYS

		a.m.						noon	p.m.													a.m.				p.m.										
DOUGLAS (Derby Castle) dep.		7 0	8 50	10 0	10 30	11 0	12 0	12 0	1 0	2 0	2 30	3 15	4 0	5 0	5 30	6 30	8 0	9 0	10 30		7 0	10 0	11 0	1 0	2 0	2 30	3 15	4 0	5 30	6 30	7 30	9 0	10 30
W. City, Majestic, Howstrake	"																boat				boat												
GROUDLE GLEN	"																car				car												
BALDRINE	"																																
GARWICK GLEN	"																																
LAXEY	"	7 30	9 15	10 30	11 0	11 30	12 30		1 30	2 30	3 0	3 45	4 30	5 30	6 0	7 0	8 30	9 30	11 0		7 30	10 30	11 30	1 30	2 30	3 0	3 45	4 30	6 0	7 0	8 0	9 30	11 0 stop
DHOON GLEN	"																																
GLEN MONA	"																																
BALLAGLASS GLEN	"																																
BALLAJORA, LEWAIGUE	"																																
RAMSEY (Plaza) arr.		8 15	10 0	11 15	11 45	12 15	1 15		2 15	3 15	3 45	4 30	5 15	6 15	6 45	7 45	9 15	10 15	11 45		8 15	11 15	12 15	2 15	3 15	3 45	4 30	5 15	6 45	7 45	8 45	10 15	

FROM RAMSEY   Extra Cars will also be run between the advertised times as required by the Traffic

		a.m.						noon	p.m.													a.m.			p.m.										
RAMSEY (Plaza) dep.		7 15	8 20		10 30	11 30	12 0	12 30	1 45	2 30	3 30	4 0	4 30	5 30	6 30	7 15	8 30	9 30	10 30		8 20		11 30	12 30	1 45	2 30	3 30	4 0	4 30	5 30	7 15	8 30	9 30
LEWAIGUE, BALLAJORA	"								boat																								
BALLAGLASS GLEN	"								car																								
GLEN MONA	"																																
DHOON GLEN	"																																
LAXEY	"	8 0	9 0	10 15	11 15	12 15	12 45		1 15	2 30	3 15	4 15	4 45	5 15	6 15	7 15	8 0	9 15	10 15	11 15 stop	9 0	10 15	12 15	1 15	2 30	3 15	4 15	4 45	5 15	6 15	8 0	9 15	10 15
GARWICK GLEN	"																																
BALDRINE	"																																
GROUDLE GLEN	"																																
Howstrake, Majestic, W. City	"																																
DOUGLAS (Derby Castle) arr.		8 30	9 30	10 45	11 45	12 45	1 15		1 45	3 0	3 45	4 45	5 15	5 45	6 45	7 45	8 30	9 45	10 45		9 30	10 45	12 45	1 45	3 0	3 45	4 45	5 15	5 45	6 45	8 30	9 45	10 45

RETURN TICKETS ARE AVAILABLE FOR BREAK OF JOURNEY AT ALL THE CHARMING GLENS EN ROUTE BOTH GOING AND RETURNING

60.   The curved crenellated parapets of the impressive viaduct flank open cross bench, 56-seater no.16, delivered from Milnes in 1898, and trailer no.49 as they approach Laxey station with the 16.30 service from Derby Castle on 8th August 2002. At the time former trailers nos 40 to 43 were converted to power cars nos 24 to 27 in 1903, no.16 was also modified with Brush bogies, hence the raised footboards at each end. It sports the green and white colour scheme introduced when the railway was nationalised in 1957. No.49 was one of six open trailers received from Milnes in 1893, starting life as no.11. So as to accommodate more power cars at the beginning of the number range, it was subsequently renumbered 23, then 28, before finally receiving its current identification. A canvas roof was added in 1904, replaced by wood ten years later, the bulkheads being an even later addition. It has seats available for 44 people. (T.Heavyside)

LAXEY

VII. Track plan of the station area.

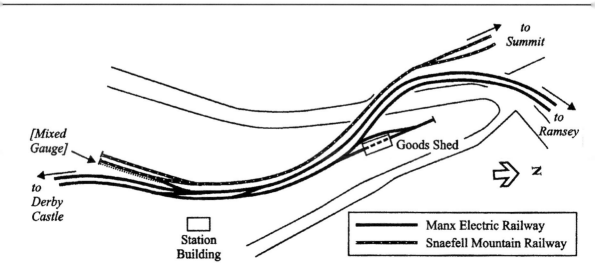

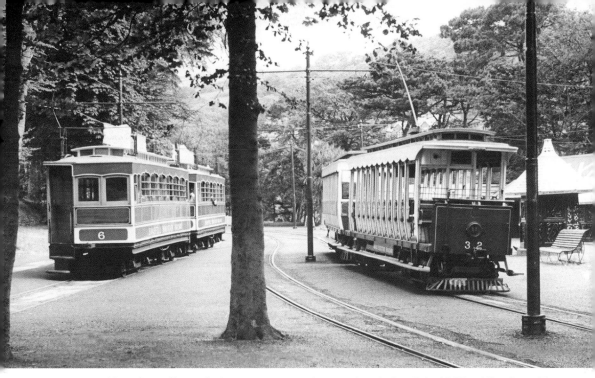

61.   No.32 and a trailer wait for custom on a pleasant day during July 1967, while alongside are two 3ft 6in gauge Snaefell Mountain Railway cars, with no.6 nearest the camera. The tracks for both railways were laid in 1898, permission having to be obtained from the Ecclesiastical Authorities for the MER rails to pass through a section of Christ Church churchyard. The church, consecrated in May 1856, is to the right of the photographer. It was originally built for the benefit of the lead miners living in the area. The corrugated iron-roofed station building on the far right has stood here since 1898. It previously served for a short time at the SMR's second terminus (see picture 66). No.6 is occupying a short length of dual gauge track laid about 1932 to facilitate the transfer of SMR stock to Derby Castle for repair and overhaul. During this exercise the SMR bodies were jacked-up while the 3ft 6in gauge axles were removed and replaced by accommodation bogies compatible with the MER 3ft 0in gauge for the trip south. Although the trackwork remains in situ, it is some years since it was last used, full maintenance facilities now being available at the SMR shed (see picture 70). (J.Fozard collection)

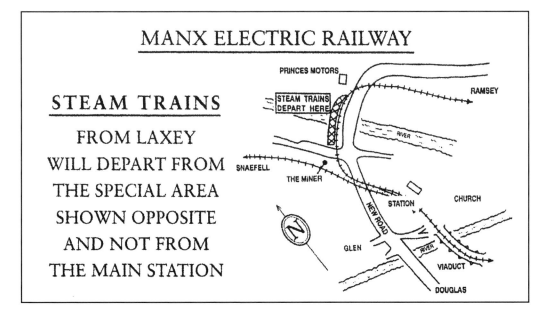

62.   At the north end of the station no.16 and attached trailer run forward prior to forming the next service to Derby Castle in September 1974. The slightly wider SMR track is on the left. The Mines Tavern, previously known as the Station Hotel and before that the home of the mine's captain, was owned by the MER prior to its sale in 1957. The goods shed beyond dates from 1903. It is now used as a store. (D.J.Mitchell)

63.   Snaefell Mountain Railway freight car no.7 'Maria', IoMR no.1 *Sutherland* and MER no.1 line up by the Mines Tavern on 21st August 1998. The former, built in 1995, is a replica of the original no.7 believed assembled in 1896 on a Milnes underframe. In common with the rest of the SMR fleet 'Maria' is fitted with two bow collectors, whereas within a few years of opening, the IoMT&EPCo opted to use trolley poles instead on the coastal route. (T.Heavyside)

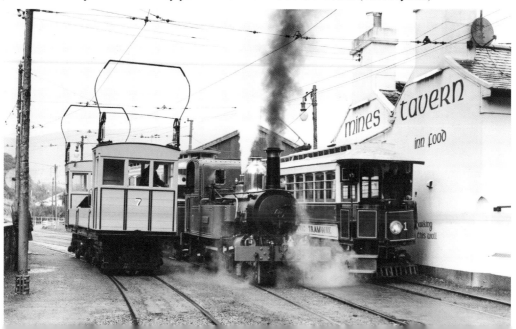

5. Snaefell Mountain Railway

The Snaefell Mountain Railway Association, a majority of whose members had strong connections with the Isle of Man Tramways & Electric Power Company, was initially responsible for this 3ft 6in gauge railway that climbs from Laxey almost to the summit of the mountain. Known for a short time as the Snaefell Mountain Tramway, it officially opened on 20th August 1895, passengers boarding the cars at a point adjacent to the present SMR car shed at Laxey. Four months later, in December 1895, the association sold its interest to the IoMT&EPCo. In 1897 a short extension enabled the cars to terminate just west of the main road through Laxey, before a second extension across the highway to the present station was brought into use the following year.

Leaving Laxey, at a mere 170ft above sea level, the line climbs the southern slope of the deep Laxey Valley as far as the Bungalow, where it crosses the A18 Douglas to Ramsey mountain road. Beyond here the railway circles around the north shoulder of the mountain, allowing first some spectacular views over Sulby Glen and reservoir, and then towards Ramsey and Point of Ayre. The terminus, a little over 4¾ miles from Laxey, is at an altitude of 1,990ft, just 46ft below the summit itself, the highest point on the island. Again Manx slate provides a solid base for the railway.

Services have always operated only during the main tourist season, in the past at peak times starting out from Laxey every 10 minutes. In recent years cars have run from the end of April until the end of September, usually at half-hourly intervals between 10.15 and 15.45 from Laxey. A Wednesday evening service was added at the height of the summer season in 2010. Journey time is 30 minutes in both directions.

VIII. Gradient profile.

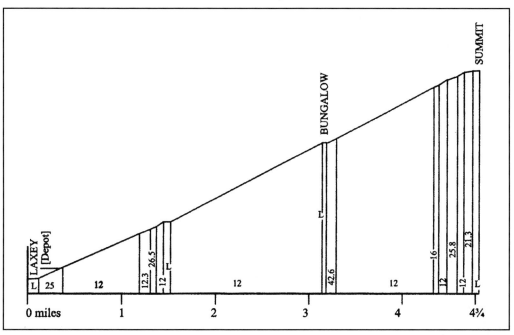

POWER CARS

Six cars, nos 1 to 6, were supplied by G.F.Milnes & Co Ltd of Birkenhead in 1895 each fitted with two bow collectors and four 25hp motors manufactured by Mather & Platt Ltd of Manchester. The overhead wire was energised at 520 volts dc, while a centre Fell Rail, originally intended as an aid to propulsion, in the event proved necessary only for braking purposes. Finished in red, white and varnished teak, the cars could accommodate 40 passengers on transverse seats plus another three in each bulkhead.

For the 1896 season the cars were fully glazed, allowing the original canvas roller blinds along each side to be dispensed with, the clerestories being added the following year. At about the same time an additional seat was installed at each end increasing the seating capacity to 48.

In about 1896 a 6-ton capacity open wagon, complete with a driving cab at each end, was put into service on an underframe obtained from Milnes. This became no.7 and was usually referred to as 'Maria'. Since normally it was only needed during the winter months in order to replenish the coal supplies at the power station near the Bungalow, it came without bogies and bow collectors. When required these had to be borrowed from one of the passenger vehicles, usually off no.5. It was little used after 1924, its condition gradually deteriorating.

The only casualty amongst the original sextet was no.5, burnt out after catching fire at the summit on 16th August 1970. A new body, without a clerestory roof and thus more akin to the original 1895 design apart from the provision of bus-type windows, was quickly manufactured by H.D.Kinnin of Ramsey. The replacement entered service in July 1971.

Over the years the sextet have retained their original livery, except for nos 2 and 4 that for a short time from the late 1950s were coated in the ill-conceived Government green and white colours following nationalisation. However, the most significant development in recent times occurred between 1977 and 1979 when the fleet was equipped with new bogies built by London Transport, together with control gear and four 61hp motors utilising materials recovered from withdrawn cars sourced at Aachen in Germany.

Four Wickham railcars, owned at various times since 1951 by the Civil Air Authority, have been the only other regular form of motive power on the mountain. They are mainly used during the winter months to access the radar station near the summit, a time when conventional cars are unable to proceed any further than the Bungalow due to the overhead wire being dismantled beyond that point. This is done annually to protect the cable from the effects of adverse weather.

No.	Builder	Year	Type	Seats	Status/Disposal
1	Milnes	1895	Vestibuled saloon	48	SMR
2	Milnes	1895	Vestibuled saloon	48	SMR
3	Milnes	1895	Vestibuled saloon	48	SMR
4	Milnes	1895	Vestibuled saloon	48	SMR
5	Milnes	1895	Vestibuled saloon	48	Body destroyed 1970 (a)
5	Kinnin	1971	Vestibuled saloon	48	SMR
6	Milnes	1895	Vestibuled saloon	48	SMR
7	Milnes	1896	Freight car	-	Remains removed
7	IoMR	1995	Freight car	-	MER (b)

Notes:
(a) Body destroyed by fire at Summit 16th August 1970
(b) Transferred to Manx Electric Railway 2003 for use as a works car

Builders:
IoMR   Isle of Man Railway, Douglas
Kinnin   H.D.Kinnin, Ramsey
Milnes   G.F.Milnes & Co Ltd, Birkenhead

LAXEY

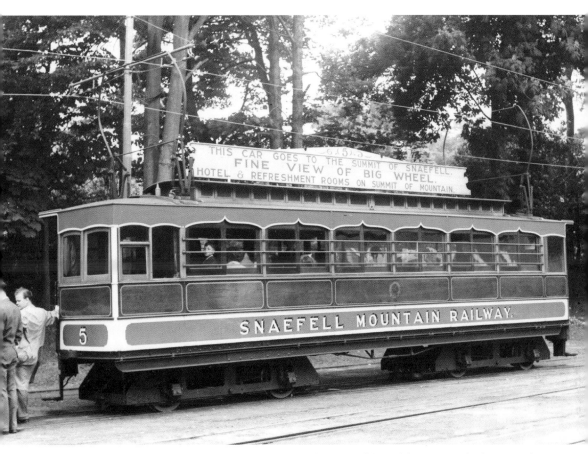

64.   A portrait of no.5 on 14th June 1958. The large roof board leaves no doubt as to its destination, along with a reminder that on the way passengers would enjoy a fine view of the 'Big Wheel' and sustenance was available, if needed, at the summit. (R.E.Gee)

MANX ELECTRIC RAILWAY   Douglas, Laxey, Ramsey & Snaefell

TIME TABLE—Saturday, 24th May, 1975 until **12th September, 1975**

Time from Derby Castle :—   THE SNAEFELL MOUNTAIN RAILWAY OPEN FROM 12th May until 26th September, 1975   CARS AS REQUIRED BY TRAFFIC
Groudle 12 mins.; Garwick 20 mins.; Dhoon 45 mins.; Ballaglass 55 mins.; Change at Laxey for the Glorious Trip to the Summit of Snaefell Mountain (2,034 feet above sea level)
The run on the Open Cars by the Direct Route to Ramsey through magnificent Woodland and Marine Scenery is of unrivalled popularity

FROM DOUGLAS		WEEKDAYS														SUNDAYS								
		B	A					noon	p.m.				B	A	A	A			p.m.		A	B	A	A
DOUGLAS (Derby Castle)	dep.	7 0		10 0	10 30	11 0	12 0	1 0	2 0	2 30	3 15	4 0	5 0	5 30	6 0	6 45	7 15	8 15	9 45	10 0	11 0	1 0	2 0	2 30	3 15	4 0	5 0	5 30	6 0	7 15	8 15	9 45
W. City, Majestic, Howstrake	,,																									
GROUDLE GLEN	,,																									
BALDRINE	,,																									
GARWICK	,,	a.m.																								
LAXEY	,,	7 30	7 30	10 30	11 0	11 30	12 30	1 30	2 30	3 0	3 45	4 30	5 30	6 0	6 30	7 15	7 45	8 45	10 15	10 30	11 30	1 30	2 30	3 0	3 45	4 30	5 30	6 0	6.30	7.45	8 45	10 15
DHOON GLEN	,,									stop		stop			stop	stop									stop			stop	stop
GLEN MONA	,,																									
BALLAGLASS GLEN	,,																									
BALLAJORA LEWAIGUE	,,																									
RAMSEY (Plaza)	arr.	8 15	8 15	11 15	11 45	12 15	1 15	2 15	3 15	3 45	4 30	5 15	6 15		7 15		8 30			11 15	12 15	2 15	3 15	3 45	4 30	5 15	6 15		7 15	8 30

Cars marked "A" operate 7th July until 22nd August   Cars marked "B" operate 24th May until 6th July also 23rd Aug. until 12th Sept.

FROM RAMSEY						noon	p.m.								p.m.									
										A	A	A								A	A
RAMSEY (Plaza)	dep.	a.m.																			
LEWAIGUE, BALLAJORA	,,	8 30		10 30	11 30	12 0	12 30	1 45	2 30	3 30	4 0	4 30	5 30	6 30		9 0		11 30	12 30	1 45	2 30	3 30	4 0	4 30	5 30	6 30		9 0
BALLAGLASS GLEN	,,																					
GLEN MONA	,,																					
DHOON GLEN	,,																					
LAXEY	,,	9 0	10 15	11 15	12 15	12 45	1 15	2 30	3 15	4 15	4 45	5 15	6 15	7 15	7 40	9 0	9 45	10 15	12 15	1 15	2 30	3 15	4 15	4 45	5 15	6 15	7 15	9 0	9 45
GARWICK	,,																					
BALDRINE	,,																					
GROUDLE GLEN	,,																					
Howstrake, Majestic, W. City	,,																					
DOUGLAS (Derby Castle)	arr.	9 30	10 45	11 45	12 45	1 15	1 45	3 0	3 45	4 45	5 15	5 45	6 45	7 45	8 10	9 30	10 15	10 45	12 45	1 45	3 0	3 45	4 45	5 15	5 45	6 45	7 45	9 30	10.15

Extra Cars will also be run between the advertised times as required by the traffic

RETURN TICKETS ARE AVAILABLE FOR BREAK OF JOURNEY AT ALL CHARMING GLENS EN ROUTE BOTH GOING AND RETURNING

1 Strathallan Crescent, Douglas. Phone Nos.: Douglas 4549 ; Laxey 226 ; Ramsey 2249.   Telegrams : Electric Douglas   **H. GILMORE, General Manager**

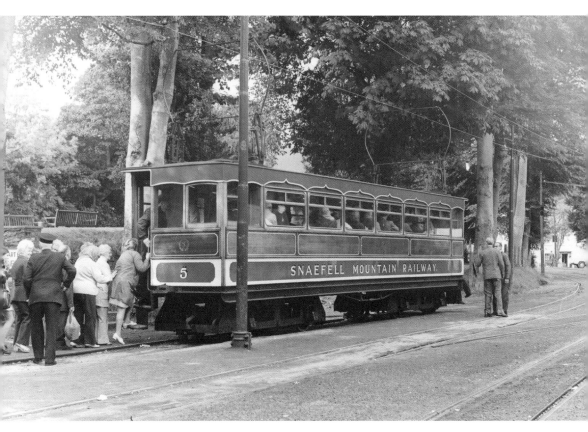

65.   The rebuilt no.5 stands in more or less the same position as the previous picture, shortly after its reinstatement in 1971. It is now without a clerestory roof, the roof board also being dispensed with, while the redesigned sliding top windows obviated the need for safety bars. Note the different style of lining, with the crest applied to the end rather than the centre side panel. (D.J.Mitchell)

↗ 66. After crossing the A2 Douglas to Ramsey road the Snaefell line veers sharply away from the MER, near what was the site of the second SMR station. Already the Laxey Wheel 'Lady Isabella' is in sight, just to the left of car no.9 approaching with a MER service from the north on 10th September 1974. The centre Fell Rail is prominent beyond the spring-loaded points, cars destined for the mountain using the right-hand track. The well-known Brown's café on the end of Dumbell's Row, popularly known as 'Ham & Egg Terrace', still serves meals, although now describing itself as a restaurant. (D.J.Mitchell)

➔   67. Access to the depot is off the descending line. No.4 has just left its night-time abode before running down to Laxey station in August 1968. This rather unusual segmented piece of trackwork was replaced by a more conventional design in 1985. (D.J.Mitchell)

WEST FROM LAXEY

SNAEFELL CAR SHED

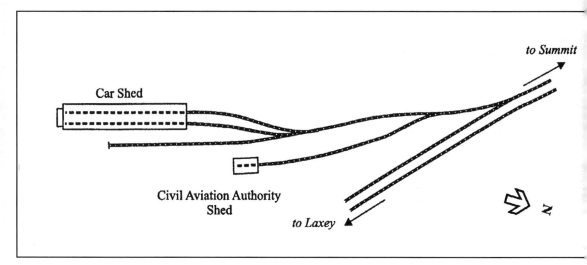

Car Shed

to Summit

Civil Aviation Authority
Shed

to Laxey

N

IX. Track plan of the site prior to completion of the new facilities in 1995.

68.　　At what was the site of t' first Laxey terminus, the fine detail of the doyen of the fleet, with no.6 behind, ca' 'died ir　ph' ʻph from 22nd June 1955. Beyond the tower wagon at the far end of the siding is the decayi　ʻuy of the original no.7 'Maria'. (H.Ballantyne)

69.		Early one morning in August 1968, four cars stand ready to proceed to Laxey station before spending yet another day toiling up and down the mountain. This two-road shed, 119ft long, 20ft 6in wide and 18ft high to the apex of the corrugated-iron roof, could accommodate all six passenger cars, although conditions were somewhat cramped. (D.J.Mitchell)

70.		A new, larger and far superior shed, with three roads under cover, was completed in 1995. With full workshop and storage space now available, the railway is effectively self-contained without the need to rely quite so much on the facilities at Derby Castle. Two Wickham railcars were ensconced in the National Air Traffic Services 'garage' on the left when photographed in September 2009. (T.Heavyside)

WEST FROM LAXEY

71.   As advertised on the boards mounted on the cars, on the lower reaches of the climb one of the island's best known features, 'Lady Isabella', is in full view. With a diameter of 72ft 6in and 6ft 0in wide it is the largest water wheel in the world. From 1854 until 1929 it pumped water at a rate of 250 gallons per minute from the lead workings nearly 2,000 feet below the surface. Named after Lady Isabella Hope, the wife of the governor in 1854, the wheel was purchased by the Manx Government in 1965 and fully restored. No.2 on the track nearest the camera, on its way down the mountain, has just passed no.1 during May 1965. (D.J.Mitchell)

72.   With snow in evidence, a Wickham railcar owned by the Ministry of Aviation, cautiously makes its way down the mountain after a service visit to the summit, on a bitterly cold 24th February 1973. (A.M.Davies)

BUNGALOW

73.   At a height of 1,355ft above sea level this is the only intermediate station. It was for a time known as Halfway. Competitors on the famed TT (Tourist Trophy) course hurtle past here at speeds of well over 100mph while heading south, away from the camera back towards Douglas on what is the A18 road from Ramsey. When racing is in progress services across the level crossing are suspended. Hidden behind the MER-owned hotel is the junction with the A14 road to Sulby and Jurby, while the slopes of Mullagh Ouyr rise in the background. From 1907 until 1953 (except for wartime years) and again in 1957 and 1958 many passengers alighted here so as to take advantage of the railway-operated charabanc service to another of the MER hotels at Tholt-y-Will in the glen below. In 1938 there was a charge of one shilling for the return trip. The Bungalow Hotel was knocked-down in 1958, a few years after this photograph was exposed at a time when MotorCycling magazine cost 8d every Thursday. (Travel Lens Photographic)

74.   After the hotel was demolished tickets could be obtained from this much more modest structure on the left, although in 1984 it was to suffer the same fate as its predecessor. No.1 pauses while on its way to the summit in May 1965. The traction poles mark the route leading towards the top of the mountain. (D.J.Mitchell)

75.   As part of the SMR centenary celebrations in 1995 former Manx Northern Railway 0-6-0T no.4 (Isle of Man Railway no.15) *Caledonia*, a product of Dübs & Co of Glasgow in 1885, returned to its haunts of 1895 when it was borrowed to assist with construction work. As no.2 resumes its journey upwards on 21st August 1995 *Caledonia* occupies a specially laid 3ft 0in gauge siding on the north side of the station. A temporary additional rail, necessary because of the gauge difference, enabled *Caledonia* to propel Manx Electric trailer no.57 up the mountain on selected dates that year. Both *Caledonia* and no.57 were temporarily fitted with brake calipers for gripping the Fell Rail. The open wagon in the right foreground utilises the siding installed in 1983 to facilitate the movement of materials during the renovation of the Summit Hotel (see picture 79). At this time the booking office was located in the small building behind *Caledonia*, otherwise used as a race marshals' hut. (J.Holroyd)

76. Since 2005 staff and passengers have benefited from this fine two-storey building incorporating the booking office, waiting area etc, erected on the site of the old hotel. No.1 is on its way back to Laxey on 24th September 2009. (T.Heavyside)

SUMMIT

SNAEFELL MOUNTAIN RAILWAY

BUNGALOW - SUMMIT
STEAM TRAIN

1.00PM

24 JUN 1995

No. 86

Up

Dn

Valid this date only

77. This substantial fortified building replaced an inadequate wooden structure in 1906. No.1 pauses before descending to Laxey in May 1939. The actual summit of the mountain, another 46ft higher than the rails, is behind the hotel, from where when conditions are favourable it is possible to see parts of England, Ireland, Scotland and Wales.
(D.J.Mitchell collection)

78. The hotel looked far less imposing in July 1955 following removal of the turrets and castellated features. Protruding above is the Air Ministry radar tower, finished in 1951. No.6 has clambered up the mountain on this occasion. (J.Fozard collection)

79. The building was ruined by fire in August 1982. The facility was reinstated in time for the 1984 season. No.1 is again present on 24th September 2009, a day of swirling mist when it was impossible to see beyond the shores of the island. With the track being more or less level there is no need for the Fell Rail near the terminus. Note, too, the unusual single-bladed point, the lever on the left protected by a barrier. (T.Heavyside)

6. Great Laxey Mine Railway

Before continuing north from Laxey, there is time for a brief visit to the latest railway attraction on the island. This 1ft 7in gauge line originally carried the raw material from the productive Laxey lead mine to the washing floors. From 1877, when they replaced ponies, two 0-4-0 steam locomotives, *Ant* and *Bee*, obtained from Stephen Lewin of Poole, Dorset, hauled the wagons. After the mine finally ceased production in 1929 the track was lifted and the two engines scrapped. Restoration work was started by the Laxey & Lonan Heritage Trust in 1999, and passenger rides commenced in 2004 along a ¼-mile length of track laid from Laxey Valley Gardens to a picnic site established near the old adit. Replicas of the 0-4-0s, ordered from Great Northern Steam Company of Darlington, arrived the same year. A battery-electric locomotive has since been acquired. The railway is usually open on Saturdays and Bank Holidays from Easter to September.

Locomotives 2010

Name	Type	Builder	Year
Wasp	4wBE	Clayton	1973 (a)
Ant	0-4-0	GNS	2004
Bee	0-4-0	GNS	2004

Note:
(a) Regauged from 1ft 6in Alan Keef Ltd, Ross-on-Wye, 2009

Builders:
Clayton   Clayton Equipment Ltd, Hatton, Derbyshire
GNS   Great Northern Steam Co Ltd, Darlington

LAXEY VALLEY GARDENS

80.   *Bee* propels the diminutive passenger carriage past the shed at the start of its journey towards the Laxey Wheel, as MER nos 22 (back in standard colours – see picture 23) and 42 pass above with the 14.40 service from Ramsey on 9th September 2006. A few seconds later *Bee* entered the restricted tunnel under the A2 road just as no.22 swung sharply round to pass overhead, behind the author, on the approach to Laxey station. (T.Heavyside)

81. *Ant* poses outside the stone-built shed on the same day. These rather unusual 0-4-0 locomotives carry their main supply of water in a semi-circular topped tank bolted to the front of the engine and held by a bracket either side of the boiler barrel. There is an additional small tank between the frames just in front of the footplate. (T.Heavyside)

→ 82. A panorama across the old washing floors as *Ant* and *Bee* attract the attention of visitors, again on 9th September 2006. At a higher level MER nos 20 and 46 begin the stiff climb towards Bulgham with the 13.10 from Derby Castle to Ramsey. (T.Heavyside)

→ 83. From 2008 the boarding point was relocated to a position parallel with the main road. The new layout was pictured on a dismal day of driving rain in September 2009. Just beyond the station limits trains must now negotiate a very tight, near 90 degree curve before entering the tunnel under the roadway. On the right is the new carriage shed. (T.Heavyside)

7. Minorca to Queen's Drive

MINORCA

84. After resuming our trip along the MER this is the first stopping place after Laxey. The corrugated iron shelter was looking rather shabby, its windows boarded-over, in this view in the direction of Ramsey on 1st July 1975. Of note are the castellated parapets of the bridge over the minor road running from the A2 down to Old Laxey. The white-painted house on the hillside, noted from South Cape in picture 53, is seen from a different perspective. (J.L.Stevenson)

↗ 85. On the afternoon of 20th January 1967, shortly after the 1.15pm from Douglas to Ramsey had passed, the embankment subsided, causing the immediate suspension of through services. A second, even more serious slip occurred on 28th January. Temporary termini were established on both sides of the effected area, and on 18th March 1967 no.21 waits to return to Douglas, while on the north side of the divide no.20 has just arrived from Ramsey. (D.J.Mitchell)

→ 86. During the reconstruction work it was also necessary to close the adjacent A2 Douglas to Ramsey road to vehicle traffic. Meanwhile, as depicted in this scene on 29th May 1967, the terminal area at the south end had been paved and steps erected up to the roadway, with a protective fence positioned on the seaward side. The wooden hut was for staff use. (D.J.Mitchell)

BULGHAM BAY

87.　For nearly six months passengers had to walk the 100 yards or so between the two terminals. Here, on the same day as the previous picture, no.7 and a trailer approach from the north. They had just passed a temporary crossover installed to facilitate the turn back procedure. As at the south end, a paved area and steps were provided for the convenience of travellers. Note the repositioned traction pole with a single bracket. (D.J.Mitchell)

→ 88. During early July, with members of the permanent way gang looking on, no.14, in use as a works car, propels a wagon over the crossover installed at the south station. At this time the stub of the southbound line, on the right, was in use as a siding. (J.Fozard collection)

→　89. Through running between Douglas and Ramsey recommenced on 10th July 1967. The spectacular nature of the surrounds can be appreciated from this lofty vantage point as nos 25 and 45, having just passed the summit some 588ft above sea level, coast downgrade towards Laxey on 10th September 1974. The train is near the site of the temporary crossover positioned to the north of the slip, while the corresponding one to the south, by the double-decker bus heading north along the A2, was left in situ. (D.J.Mitchell)

90.   This slightly raised platform was laid in the summer of 2009 and sees occasional use by special charter trips when stops are made for photography purposes. There is no access from the road. Nos 22 and 40 hurry by with the 11.10 departure from Ramsey on 24th September 2009. (T.Heavyside)

↗ 91. On 19th May 1959 no.19 rounds the sharp curve with a northbound service and prepares to halt to enable any would-be visitors to the 44-acre, steep-sided glen to alight. The MER once rented the glen, making a modest charge for admission. On the opposite side of the A2 stood a railway-owned hotel until April 1932, when it was ravaged by fire. The area occupied by the latter, to the right of the photographer, is now a car park. (A.D.Packer)

→ 92. The old waiting shelter was removed in 1985, a new, improved version appearing in 1987. It is seen to advantage as no.19 approaches from Ramsey on 28th April 2001. The glen is now designated a National Glen and in 2007 was awarded the status of an Area of Special Scientific Interest due to the many rare fauna and flora to be found along its length. (T.Heavyside)

DHOON GLEN

DHOON QUARRY

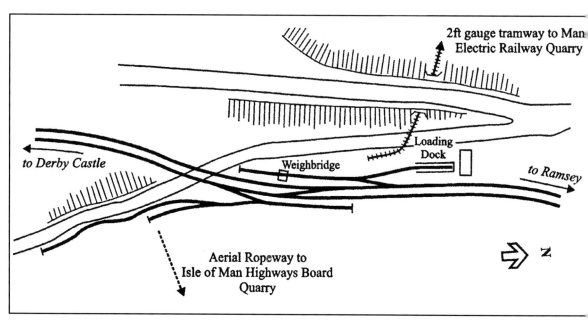

X. Track plan of the site in the days when stone quarrying had an important role.

93. This was once a very busy place despatching the output from two nearby quarries. The stone from the MER's own quarry, on the west side of the railway, was carried to the sidings by a 2ft gauge tramway, while on the opposite side of the line an aerial ropeway conveyed the produce excavated from the Highways Board's quarry. These activities had ceased by the mid-1930s, the area subsequently being utilised by the permanent way department. Hundreds of sleepers were stacked at the south end of the site on 30th August 1961, while parked in the siding were a trio of 6-ton capacity wagons, nos 5, 7 and 8, built by Milnes between 1896 and 1898. No.5 has since been scrapped. Until comparatively recent times, near the end of the siding, was a weighbridge by H.Pooley & Son Ltd of Liverpool & London, similar to the one at Peel manufactured by the same company (see *Douglas to Peel* picture 111). The building in the centre of the picture, 'creosote cottage', was cleared in 1979/80, although the old smithy to be seen on the left remains extant. (J.L.Stevenson)

94.   Here the revitalised centre-cab no.23 commands attention as it hauls a demonstration freight consisting of wagon no.8 and van no.14 back to Laxey on 30th May 1983. The locomotive in its original form can be seen in picture 16. After suffering damage in 1914 it was rebuilt in 1925 and, together with the bodies of two 6-ton wagons, mounted on a new underframe, giving an increased overall length of 34ft 6in although its maximum height was reduced by 1ft to 10ft 0in. When required the bogies from under car no.33 were borrowed. It was stored from 1944 until cosmetically restored in 1978 for display in Ramsey Tram Museum (see picture 114), before being returned to working order in 1983. (J.L.Stevenson)

ISLE OF MAN RAILWAYS

Steam Train on the Manx Electric Railway

1 RETURN JOURNEY

№ 1919

Depart Laxey   12-45

Date   -4 SEP 1993
VALID THIS DATE ONLY

Issued subject to the Department's Conditions of Carriage

95.   During another gala event ten years later, MER centenary year, IoMR 2-4-0T no.4 *Loch* (Beyer Peacock works no.1416 of 1874) was utilised on a series of shuttles from Laxey hauling MER trailers nos 57 and 58. After the exertions of the climb over Bulgham summit on 28th June 1993, *Loch* takes a well-earned breather in the siding occupied by the wagons in picture 93. On the left trailer no.48 brings up the rear of a southbound service. The bunting adds to the festive nature of the occasion. (A.D.Packer)

96.   In recent years a large scale track renewal programme has been undertaken by outside contractors. Early in 2006 Ruston & Hornsby 0-6-0DM *Bertie*, built 1949, was hired by RMS Locotec of Wakefield to assist the movement of materials etc. During its early years *Bertie* was used by the cement industry, but prior to being moved to the island had been preserved at the Irchester Country Park in Northamptonshire. Since its arrival five 4-wheeled diesels have also been acquired from Bord Na Mona – the Irish Turf Board for similar duties, although one has been scrapped. *Bertie* is seen nearest the camera, next to the chassis of former passenger trailer no.45 on 24th September 2009. Also on view are three of the ex-Bord Na Mona locos and, at the far end of the siding, three side-tipping wagons. (T.Heavyside)

GLEN MONA

97.　　This southward view was obtained on 28th June 1975. MER staff would only collect the letters deposited in the pillar-box for a further three months. The shelter was dismantled in 1987. (J.L.Stevenson)

98.　　In 1988 a new shelter replaced the earlier example. It is seen here, with the nameboard attached to the roof, on what was a warm summer's afternoon in late June 1993. No.20 is about to stop with a service from Ramsey. The former postal facility has been moved elsewhere. (A.D.Packer)

BALLAGORRY

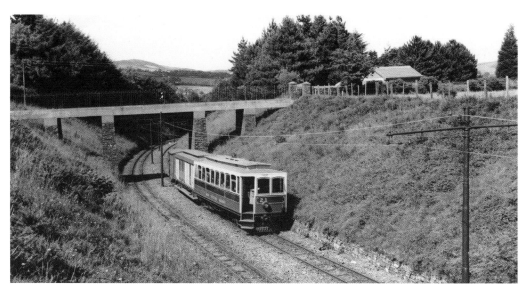

99.   No.21, with a trailer and van in tow, hastens south having just passed beneath what is now the only bridge over the MER on 21st July 1960 (the comparatively short-lived footbridge at Derby Castle was the only other example - see pictures 7 and 11). This concrete footbridge, resting on stone pillars, replaced a wooden structure in 1950. In 1989 a new electricity sub-station was installed under the bridge, superseding the power station at nearby Ballaglass. (A.D.Packer)

BALLAGLASS GLEN

100.   The   nameboard is above the entrance to the glen, another of those once owned by the MER. The motorman in charge of no.32, accompanied by trailer no.62, heading for Douglas on 6th August 1968, is about to apply the brakes. The design of this 56-seater cross bench open provides an ideal driving position on warm sunny days. (J.L.Stevenson)

CORNAA

101. A solitary lady passenger makes her way towards the platform of Douglas-bound 'Winter Saloon' no.19 on a rather bleak, unseasonable day in August 1974. The station name is displayed prominently above the waiting shelter, the words in smaller type reminding intending travellers that this is a 'Request Stop'. In the days before mass car ownership, the MER provided a vital lifeline for some of the rural communities in the north of the island. (A.M.Davies)

DAILY SATURDAY 1 APRIL TO SUNDAY 29 OCTOBER

DOUGLAS - GROUDLE - LAXEY - MAUGHOLD - RAMSEY

		B				B		D			A	C	C	C
DOUGLAS, Derby Castle	0945	1015	1045	1145	1245	1345	1415	1445	1515	1615	1715	1815	1950	2115
Groudle	0957	1027	1057	1157	1257	1357	1427	1457	1527	1627	1727	1827	2002	2127
Baldrine	1003	1033	1103	1203	1303	1403	1433	1503	1533	1633	1733	1833	2008	2133
South Cape	1010	1040	1110	1210	1310	1410	1440	1510	1540	1640	1740	1840	2015	2140
Laxey	1015	1045	1115	1215	1315	1415	1445	1515	1545	1645	1745	1845	2020	2145
Dhoon	1030	1100	1130	1230	1330	1430	1500	1530	1600	1700	1800			
Ballaglass	1040	1110	1140	1240	1340	1440	1510	1540	1610	1710	1810			
Ballajora	1048	1118	1148	1248	1348	1448	1518	1548	1618	1718	1818			
RAMSEY, Tram Station	1100	1130	1200	1300	1400	1500	1530	1600	1630	1730	1830			

A - Runs 1 May to 1 October ONLY
B - Runs 29 May to 10 September ONLY
C - Runs Monday to Saturday 17 July to 26 August ONLY
D - Runs Monday to Thursday 17 July to 24 August ONLY

ACCORDING TO DEMAND, EXTRA TRAMS MAY RUN PARTICULARLY BETWEEN DOUGLAS AND LAXEY

Illuminated Tram - Groudle Shuttle

Tuesdays 1, 8, 15 August. Wednesdays 5 July to 16 August.

in connection with Groudle Glen Railway Evening Services					
Douglas	1845	1915	1945	2015	2045
Groudle	1857	1927	1957	2027	2057
Groudle	1900	1930	2000	2030	2115
Douglas	1912	1942	2012	2042	2127

Intermediate stops are BY REQUEST except Groudle and Laxey. TO ALIGHT inform conductor on boarding. TO BOARD give clear hand signal to driver.

DAILY MONDAY 17 APRIL TO SUNDAY 1 OCTOBER

LAXEY - SNAEFELL SUMMIT

Regular departures from Laxey Station between 1015 and 1545 (last guaranteed ascent)
Journey time 30 minutes each way. Refreshments and licensed bar available at Summit Hotel.
Services operate subject to weather conditions

BALLAJORA

102.   The Victorian letterbox and the corrugated iron shelter of similar vintage are prominent in this panorama looking south on 28th June 1975. The photographer was standing on the A15 road. This serves Maughold in the form of a loop off the A2, the two junctions being about 1½ miles apart. (J.L.Stevenson)

DREEMSKERRY

103.   This picturesque spot is enhanced by nos 7 and 43 as they prepare to call to collect a lone passenger while heading south on 28th August 1961. Not long after leaving the halt, the train will pass near the site of a former quarry that was once a source of valued income for the MER. (J.L.Stevenson)

LEWAIGUE

104.   The nameboard proclaims this to be yet another request stop. Looking in the direction of Ramsey on 28th June 1975, we see the shelter destroyed by vandals in 1986, as was the nameboard a few years later. Both have been replaced. The cast iron pedestal box, in front of traction pole no.811, originally contained feeder equipment for the overhead along with switchgear for isolation purposes. The script lettering on the box 'IMT&EPCo' harks back to the very early days of the railway. (J.L.Stevenson)

BELLE VUE

105.   A couple of ladies prepare to board either no.20 or its trailer for the short journey to Ramsey on 19th August 1961. At the rear is 6-ton van no.16, built by the MER in 1908. Presumably a strong westerly wind was blowing, since for the comfort of passengers most of the curtains on the landward side of the trailer have been drawn down. Beyond the train, the Queen's Pier at Ramsey stretches out into the Irish Sea, while in the far distance the Ayre Peninsula points towards the Scottish coastline. (J.L.Stevenson)

106.   Down at track level on 28th June 1975, we are able to take a closer look at this stopping place from the A15 roadway. It will be noted the halt is also known as Port-e-Vullen (Port of the Mill) after a small bay nearby. The postbox and the shelter are no more, a much more modest wooden version having replaced the latter in recent years. (J.L.Stevenson)

BALLURE VIADUCT

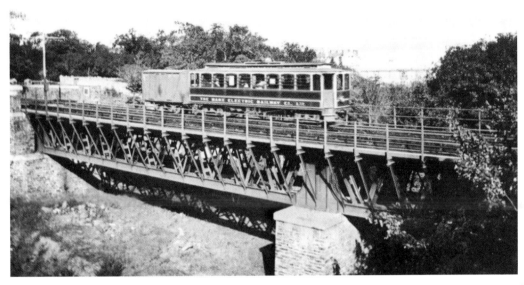

107.   In this postcard view from about 1912, Ramsey Pier can be glimpsed beyond the trees as a power car and trailing van ride high over Ballure Glen on their way south. This 160ft-long girder bridge, with a central column for support, was finished in July 1899. As plaques bear witness, it was manufactured and erected by Francis Morton & Co Ltd, bridge and roof builders of Garston (Liverpool), W.L.Knowles being the engineer. Prior to completion, trains used a temporary terminus on the south side of the glen from August 1898. (J.D.Darby collection)

108.   With trees obscuring the floor of the valley, nos 6 and 46 stride over the viaduct, having just crossed over the A2 road on their way out of Ramsey. Since 1936 the level crossing has been protected by colour-light signals activated by approaching trains. Speed across the bridge is restricted to 5mph. (J.L.Stevenson)

QUEEN'S DRIVE

109.   In the suburbs of Ramsey, a Vauxhall Viva waits at the junction of Queen's Drive with Walpole Road as no.19 traverses a short section of grooved rail, soon after the start of its journey to Douglas on 10th September 1974. Ornate single bracket traction poles, on the landward side of the tracks, are a feature between here and Walpole Drive, a requirement of Ramsey Commissioners when the railway was built. Note the supply of new rails stored on the left. (D.J.Mitchell)

8. Ramsey Pier Tramway

Just a short walk from the MER Queen's Drive stop is the 2,160ft-long Queen's Pier (sometimes referred to as 'The Iron Pier') at the south end of the promenade. When opened in 1886, a 3ft 0in gauge tramway was provided to convey luggage to and from the steamers that berthed at the pier head. However, the trolleys had to be pushed by hand, as had a passenger car introduced a few years later. In 1937 internal combustion power replaced brute force. Steamers ceased to call at Ramsey from 1970, after which the tramway operated spasmodically until 1981. The pier closed to the public in 1991 and now stands derelict and forlorn, although restoration plans have been drawn up with a view to eventual reopening.

110.   The Wickham railcar, transported from the mainland in 1950, sets off seaward in the summer of 1967. Business appears brisk on this occasion with the 10-seater car full to capacity. The Isle of Man Harbour Board charged 4d (children half price) for a single journey. (D.J.Mitchell)

111.   Looking towards the pier entrance in September 1974, Hibberd 'Planet' 4-wheel petrol locomotive no.2027, built in 1937, and the 15-seater passenger car shipped to the island at the same time are prominent. The Wickham railcar, then known as the 'Galloping Goose' as inscribed above the front windows, stands between the kiosks by the entrance. The Queen's Hotel offered splendid sea views until its closure following a fire in 1983, as do the apartments now occupying the site. Trinity United Reform Church, seen on the right, continues to serve the community. (D.J.Mitchell)

112.   The pier was photographed from the promenade on 24th September 2009. Today, the legend 'Queen's Pier' remains emblazoned in bold letters above the securely locked entrance. A couple of plaques, mounted one each side of the gateway, proudly proclaim that 'King Edward VII and Queen Alexandra landed here August 25 1902' and 'King George V and Queen Mary also landed here July 14 & 15 1920'. Although the landing stage at the far end has been dismantled, the rails along the pier are still embedded in the decking, while the Planet locomotive and passenger car can be seen in the Manx Transport Museum at Jurby. It opened in 2010. (T.Heavyside)

9. Ramsey

RAMSEY CAR SHED

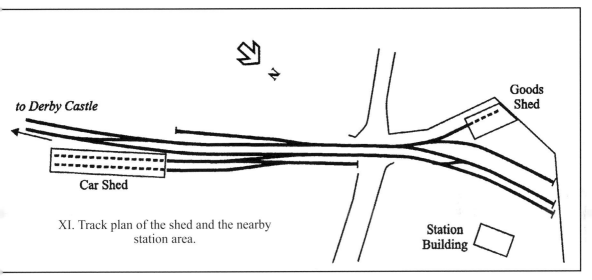

to Derby Castle

Car Shed

XI. Track plan of the shed and the nearby
station area.

Goods
Shed

Station
Building

113.   At the end of its turn of duty on 2nd August 1962, 'Tunnel Car' no.9 prepares to enter the 1899-erected wood and corrugated iron two-road shed, where it will spend the night. On the right are nos 21 and 41, the latter one of a trio of 1930-built trailers that replaced those lost in the Laxey fire that same year. They decelerate as they travel the last few yards towards the terminus with a service from Douglas. 'Winter Saloon' no.21 is 7ft 4in wide while the noticeably narrower no.9 measures only 6ft 3in. (J.L.Stevenson)

114.   For the Manx Millennium celebrations in 1979, the building was converted to a tram museum. Exhibited in pristine condition during its opening year were steeple-cab no.23 after a cosmetic restoration the previous year, and freight vehicle no.26. The latter had previously languished for many years in a rather sorry state inside Laxey car shed (see picture 55). The poster on the left refers to another of the large exhibits, trailer no.59. This was built specially by Milnes in 1895 for use of the directors. It has open platforms and can seat 18 people. Originally this 22ft 2in long trailer only had four wheels, bogies being fitted in 1900. On 25th August 1902, during the visit to the island referred in picture 112, King Edward VII and Queen Alexandra travelled from Derby Castle to Walpole Road aboard no.59, since when it has often been referred to as the 'Royal Saloon'. (J.L.Stevenson)

115.   In 1993 the shed resumed its intended role. The front and west elevations, along with the backs of properties on Waterloo Road, can be studied, as no.20 begins the climb away from Ramsey with the 14.40 service to Derby Castle on 28th April 2001. Goods van no.14, standing in the old cattle dock siding, is adorned with a somewhat out-of-date advertising sign! (T.Heavyside)

RAMSEY

116.   The rather unpretentious surrounds of our destination present a complete contrast with much of what has gone before on our journey from Douglas. Here no.20 hauls a trailer and van across Parsonage Road as they depart for the south in May 1965. The track on the right forms the headshunt for the car shed, while the points in the foreground lead to the siding depicted in the previous picture. The board by the boundary wall reminds visitors to the town of the many attractions to be enjoyed in Mooragh Park. (D.J.Mitchell)

117.   Van no.3 has been left on the south side of Parsonage Road while bags of parcels and post are loaded in March 1966. This is one of the oldest freight vehicles on the MER, having been delivered from Milnes in 1894/1895. It was designed to carry loads of up to 6 tons. Behind the Royal Mail Morris Minor 1000 van is the 1903-built goods shed. It was to serve as the car shed from 1979, then as a MER visitor centre from 1993, but since 2003 has been a venue for the local youth, known as 'The Shed'. (D.J.Mitchell)

→ 118.Prior to the termination of the mail contract in September 1975, 4-wheeled goods vans could often be found stabled around the station area, as were nos 4, 12 and 14 on 30th June 1973. All three were constructed by Milnes between 1894 and 1904. No.4 on the left has similar dimensions to no.3 seen in the previous picture, and although no.12 (on the right) likewise has a 6 ton capacity it is to a much more compact design. Both these vans have end platforms, the latter with a ridged rather than an arched roof. Sandwiched between is the noticeably smaller no.14 with a reduced capacity of 5 tons. Today the chassis of no.12 supports a tower wagon while the roof and sides of no.14 were removed in 2002. (J.L.Stevenson)

→ 119.   Overshadowed by what was once the Palace Concert Hall, latterly the Plaza Cinema, nos 19 and 48 (both built 1899) wait for custom on 10th September 1974. The building was owned by the MER until 1938. The car shed can be glimpsed beyond the roadway. (D.J.Mitchell)

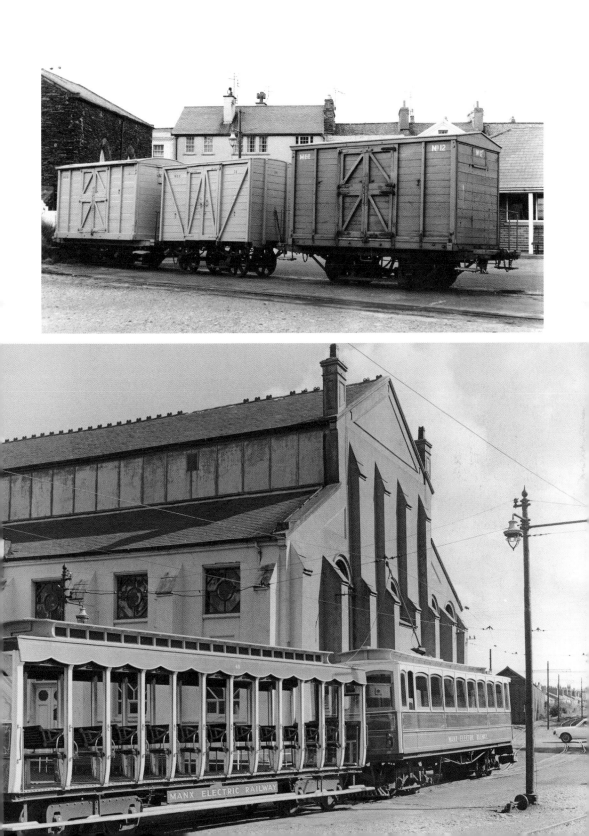

120.   Demolition of the cinema in 1991 created a much more open aspect, the inevitable car park now occupying this area. No.19 was observed shunting trailer no.40 from a standpoint close to that of picture 116 on 2nd July 1999. That year the MER was celebrating the centenary of its opening to Ramsey, no.19 carrying a commemorative headboard and with the legend 'Douglas, Laxey & Ramsey Electric Tramway' painted in large letters along the sides. (T.Heavyside)

→ 121. As passengers make their way from the ticket office, of 1964, car no.20 stands ready to form the 14.40 service to Douglas on 28th April 2001. Behind is the imposing Quayle's Hall, in use as a Presbyterian Chapel from the 1830s, and then as a Temperance Hall from 1886. Following some recent renovation work the hall has been used to stage the occasional exhibition. (T.Heavyside)

→ 122. The terminal building is seen from Albert Road on the same day as the previous picture, with a reminder of centenary year still evident. For passengers travelling in the opposite direction this is their first view of the railway, giving little indication of the remarkable journey to follow. (T.Heavyside)

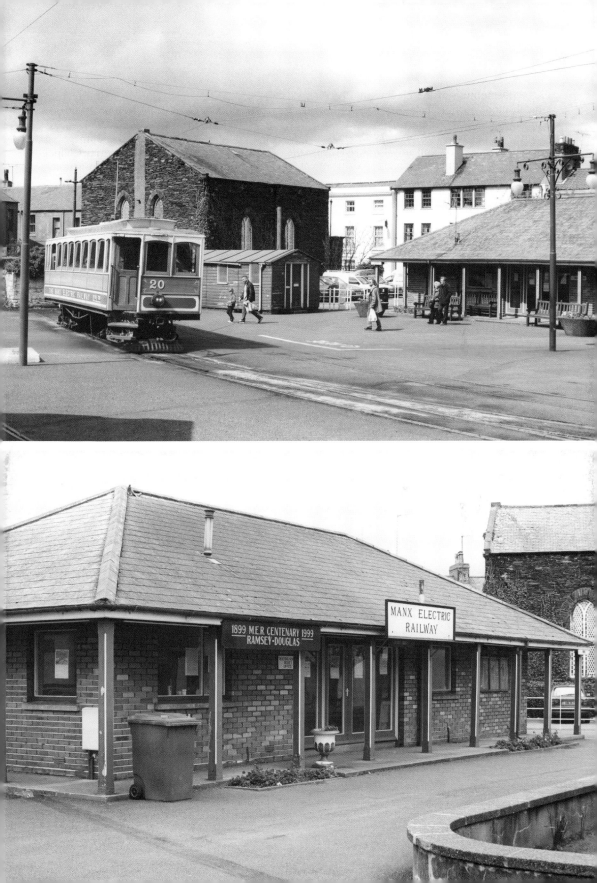

MP Middleton Press

Easebourne Lane, Midhurst, West Sussex.
GU29 9AZ   Tel:01730 813169

EVOLVING THE ULTIMATE RAIL ENCYCLOPEDIA

www.middletonpress.co.uk   email:info@middletonpress.co.uk
A-978 0 906520   B-978 1 873793   C-978 1 901706   D-978 1 904474   E-978 1 906008

All titles listed below were in print at time of publication - please check current availability by looking at our website - *www.middletonpress.co.uk* or by requesting a Brochure which includes our *LATEST* RAILWAY TITLES also our TRAMWAY, TROLLEYBUS, MILITARY and WATERWAYS series